Logo Design in Branding

Design Guide to
Typeface and Graphic

LOGO DESIGN IN BRANDING
——DESIGN GUIDE TO TYPEFACE AND GRAPHIC

ACS⌐ ⌈ARTPOWER⌐

Edited and produced by Artpower International Publishing Co., Ltd.
Address: Flat B5 1/F, Manning Ind. Bldg., 116-118 How Ming St., Kwun Tong, Kowloon, Hong Kong, China
Tel: 852-23977886
Fax: 852-23982111

www.artpower.com.cn
contact@artpower.com.cn (Editorial)
book@artpower.com.cn (Sales - China)
overseasales@artpower.com.cn (Sales - International)

ISBN 978-988-18799-6-7

Publisher: Lu Jican
Chief Editor: Zhou Ziqing
Executive Editor: Xu Kexin, Li Kun
Art Designer: Chen Ting
Cover Design: Xiong Libo
Translator: Wang Yue

Size: 185mm X 250mm
First Edition: January, 2023

Printed and bound in China.

PREFACE

Typography is a beautiful art form we all get to experience in daily life. It also plays a pivotal role in the creation of successful brands acting as an anchor for the many ways a brand comes to life in our physical & digital worlds. People respond to type on a subconscious level. Thoughtful type that reflects a brand vision & values has the ability to communicate layers of meaning. Through small subtle details, type choices affect how we feel and think about a brand.

This curation of typography and branding examples from around the world offers a global perspective on the current type landscape. This book provides valuable insights for designers and anyone who are interested in the foundations of branding. In today's highly digital world, it also offers a perspective that your personal online algorithm might not. Take time, live with the content contained within the pages of this book, ultimately you will have a deeper experience.

Typography has a very long and rich history. However in recent years we've seen the rise of many template-driven services in the design space. On one hand it has helped raise the overall standard of design, but on the other hand, it also resulted in a feeling of homogeneity and inauthenticity. In contrast, we're seeing a renaissance of independent type foundries indicating designers and ultimately society continue to place an importance role on the thoughtful well-crafted type. In combination with innovative ideas, typography will continue to provide us with great outcomes in the brand-design space. I can't wait to see what comes next!

Fredericus L'AMI
Founder, STUDIO L'AMI

We live in a visual world.

Sight is the main sense we use to perceive reality around us. Hence visual identity is one of the most important customer touch points for a company as it has the power to involve, inspire and create bonds with people. As designers, our aim is to graphically express the true essence of a brand via logo designing.

We take it very seriously at Okta Branding because we believe that it serves as a bridge between our clients and their audience. In order to build a solid connection, we must enrich our repertoire, since good aesthetic sense and a sophisticated look are essential.

Logo Design for Beginners is a refined curation that amazes us with inspiring visual identity projects from different cultures brilliantly crafted by the best agencies around the globe. It's a visual gold mine for any designer!

Camila Chisini
Founder and Director of Okta Branding

CONTENTS

Chapter 1
LOGO DESIGN FOR BRAND

1 The Importance of the Visual Design of a Brand

Philip Kotler, the father of modern marketing, defined brand in *Marketing: An Introduction*. Brand is a series of specific characteristics, benefits and services that sellers provide to buyers for a long period. An impressive brand can bring intangible assets such as brand premium and value-added to the owner, and the source of these value-added is based on the consumer's impression of the brand.

Logo is not only the external appearance of a brand, but also the clues for consumers to obtain the first impression. Placed at a vital position in the field of graphic design, Logo design is a necessary skill for designers and the first choice for greenhands.

Moreover, Logo design is in great demand, which lies not only in those newly-registered companies, but also, with the development of the enterprise and upgrading of the brand, in the brands that require to update on account of the factors such as time, market, public aesthetics, and etc. For example, Apple's Logo has developed for more than half a century, changing from the original complicated one to the classic simple one.

| 1976 | 1977 - 1998 | 1998 | 1998 - 2000 | 2001 - 2007 | Current |
| By Ron Wayne | By Rob Janoff | Translucent Version | Monochrome Version | Aqua Version | Chrome Version |

The core of Logo design lies in sparkling consumers' cognition towards the brand value. The choice of each design element in the Logo shall convey the style of the brand and attract the target consumers through design.

A well-designed Logo can reflect how the enterprises appreciate the external images, at the same time, it conveys the consumers a sense of reliability, enabling the brand to gain the popularity rapidly among the consumers and users. The standard for evaluating the Logo quality is very simple, that is, whether the general public can obtain a correct understanding of the brand from the Logo design according to their own aesthetic standards without acknowledging the brand in advance.

The Logo design involves complete graphic knowledge. The graphic patterns, font design, colour psychology, typography, etc., all will be reflected in the Logo design. Besides, Logo design can also be extended to other design-related fields, such as brand design, packaging design and advertisement design. If one starts from learning the most basic Logo design, when he turns to other fields, it would be handier and easier.

2 Direction and Pattern of Logo Manifestation

There are various Logo design techniques, which can be summarised into two "three": three directions of manifestation and three patterns of manifestation.

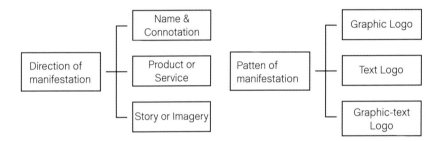

2.1 Direction of Manifestation

The Direction of Logo manifestation can be easily understood, which is nothing more than a direct reflection of the brand name, product, story. It could be the full name or the initials of English name.

Text Logo is also very common, since it is succinct and direct. One can read directly at one glance. Ellas, Format Bar, and Maldini Studios are Logos based on font design.

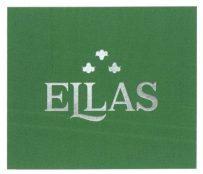

Design Agency: Bullseye

Design Agency: Funky Press

Usage in different scenarios can be satisfied by extracting the initials, such as the "M" of Maldini Studios.

Designer: Jens Nilsson

Brands related to tea often put tea leaves images in their Logos. Matchaki is a New York-based matcha promotion organization. In addition to retaining the brand's initial letter M in the Logo, the shape of the tea leaves is simplified into geometric figures, then four leaves are combined together by applying the repeated design principle.

For brands that do not have a exact product to use, the story or imagery behind them can be used as a starting point for the design. For example, the Logo of Somos organisation mentioned previously contains two "S" in the shape of hand in hand, which means "collaboration".

Design Agency: Monajans

Designer: Tomomi Maezawa

2.2 Pattern of Manifestation

From the both Chinese and international logo cases, it is not difficult to find out that people's perception always starts from the name, assisting with the specific graphics, when it comes to the content of the Logo. Therefore, the patten of Logo manifestation can be generally classified into three forms: Graphic Logo, Text Logo, and Graphic-text Logo.

For example, the Logo of Apple and of Nike, which are regarded as classic, impress people with their single graphic Logo; Coca-Cola and Google are remembered by their plain text Logos. Graphic-text Logo includes that of Huawei, Baidu, Adidas, etc., among them, graphics and text have different combine in different ways.

In most cases, Party A's attitude towards the tendency for the patten of logo manifestation ranges like this from the view of usage:

Graphic-text > Text > Graphic

Text Logo is more favorable because the Logo itself speaks for the company, which is more universal and less subject to taboos. The usage of graphics can underline the characteristics of the industry or the brand apart from answering the question "WHO AM I".

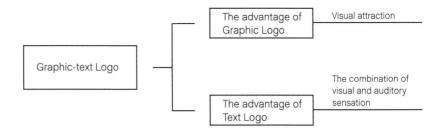

| Graphic-text Logo | The advantage of Graphic Logo | Visual attraction |
| | The advantage of Text Logo | The combination of visual and auditory sensation |

There is a process for users to understand the core values of a brand, and it takes time and communication. In terms of design alone, choosing a minimalistic Logo is risky for a not so well-known company or brand. It is not recommended for designers to follow in the earlier stage because the brand name cannot be conveyed by graphics. Moreover, the interpretation from graphics to text requires understanding, whose process cannot be controlled. Therefore, whether readers can accurately understand the meaning of the graphic Logo remains unknown.

2.2.1 Graphic Logo

The difficulty in designing the graphic Logo lies in the visualisation, that is how to turn the abstract into the figurative. There are still many options as well as the basic design key points are mastered. For example, the choice of graphics can be a plant, an animal or a portrait of the founder. If the brand emphasises the story behind it, extract elements from the story to evoke common memory of certain abstract meaning.

Graphic logo can be roughly classified into five categories, which are Botanical, Animal, Portrait, Object and Geometric. These five categories will be explained in detail in other chapters of this book.

Designer: Christian Baun

Designer: Christian Baun

2.2.2 Text Logo

Text Logo is applied widely without the restriction of specific industry. Design can start directly with the full name of the brand, or the initials or consonants of the brand name.

The text Logo of the Weightstone Vineyard Estate & Winery selects the initials of the brand name. it is dominated by "W", with "S" incorporated in.

Design Agency: 2tigers Design Studio

At the beginning of its operation, Lacoco Coffee was a store focusing on coconut milk, and "La Coco" means "coconut". Later, the shop began to sell other products such as coffee as the business scope changed. Although the name has "coconut" in it, the change in scope makes it not suitable to choose the design method of product visualisation.

Design Agency: Akronim

Therefore, the designer would like to choose the consonants of the brand name, making the Logo look clearer and simpler, which also corresponds to the principles of memorability, recognizability and succinctness.

 株式会社
浅野・出江建築事務所

Design Agency: Cosydesign

Design Agency: Notorius Grey

2.2.3 Graphic-text Logo

The graphic-text Logo, combining the advantage of graphic Logo with text one, is a mainstream in design. Apart from the Logo with graphics on the top of text, this type also integrates the graphics into text, or with text forming graphics, or fill the text with graphics.

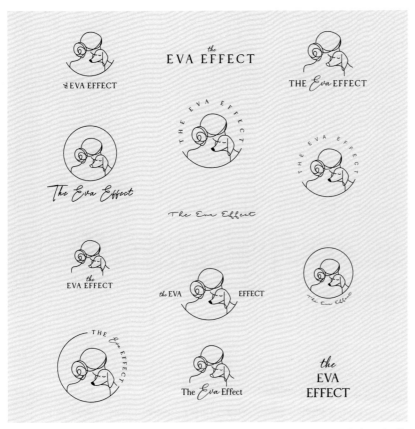

Designer: AguWu

3 Principles of Logo Design

Paul Rand, a famous American graphic designer, proposed seven inspiring and instructive design principles: memorability, uniqueness, recognisability, adaptability, universality, foresight and succinctness.

These principles are used as references, therefore not each of them is required to be satisfied. You can start with these 7 design principles, analysing the works of predecessors and reflecting on your own works. Also, you can improve your design ability through reviewing. When you hit the bottleneck, go over the 7 principles of Logo design, maybe you can gain new solutions.

(1) Memorability

The ultimate question that Logo meets is "who you are", while making it memoizable is the supreme goal. For an enterprise, the design of the Logo directly affects the public's attention and cognition of the brand. A good design allows consumers to immediately associate the brand with the logo when they have a need for a relevant product.

The first thing you need to understand is that a Logo itself is meaningless. It only makes sense when integrating with products, concepts and services over time. Nowadays, there are many websites that generate Logos online. However, no matter how well-designed they are, they are just icons, meaningless and inanimate without connecting with the brand.

(2) Uniqueness

People always prioritize unique things in memory. In short, the more special, the more profound. The uniqueness of a Logo refers to its distinctive features that make it stand out from other Logos of the same type, attracting and influencing people by strong and unique visual effects, so as to leave a deep impression on the viewer. For example, circle and ellipse are common typography in certain industry, therefore, designers can consider designing them into squares or triangles.

Uniqueness principle is the most difficult one to achieve in Logo design, since it requires designers to accumulate a large number of cases, including works from different industries and styles. The designers need to clarify which design style or method is in vogue, and what changes can be made on this basis.

For example, Somos, an NGO, is related to the arts and crafts industry. When you enter "NGO Logo" in a search engine, most of the Logos appear in bold letters, hoping to convey a sense of stability and reliability. Somos, on the other hand, interprets "friendship" in simple and clean style.

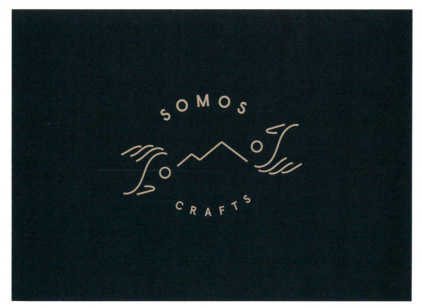

Designer: Tomomi Maezawa

(3) Recognizability

Recognizability put emphasis on the recognition of the Logo, that is to say, it must be highly recognizable, matched, simple and clear without being sloppy on the basis of meeting Party A's needs. The core of Logo design lies in sparkling consumers' cognition towards the brand value. when the brand "recognition" is emphasised, we shall recognize the Logo before understanding it. If a Logo lacks recognizability, it is very difficult to "recognize", let alone "understanding".

The choice of Logo font, the deformation of strokes, the design of the positive and negative space, and the weight of the font, especially the sharpness of font after zooming out, all will affect the recognizability of the font. Some designers will combine graphics and fonts, then questions related to the recognizability of the Logo comes again, for instance, whether the font still retains its original characteristics, or whether the typesetting order of the font will affect the reading.

Text Logo generally does not make much changes to its structure, but mostly changes the strokes, so as to maintain the recognizability of the font. Seal script, cursive script, decorative letters, gothic script, etc., which are unfamiliar with public, should be applied as little as possible. Of course, if there are special requirements, appropriate adjustments can be made to make it more understandable to the public. In addition, cool and unconventional designs may increase the cost of reading and reduce the recognition of the Logo. Remember that don't design for design's sake, and strike the balance between individuality and recognition.

(4) Adaptability

Adaptability refers to whether the Logo can be applied to various scenarios, giving full play to the cognitive characteristics of symbols on offline materials such as T-shirts, cups, packaging and online media such as App icons and web banners. Therefore, when making proposals, designers need to imagine the usage scenarios of the Logo for the client, not just simply hand in a file. The Logo must be extensible, that is, zooming in or out will not affect its recognizability.

(5) Universality

Universality refers to whether the meaning conveyed by the Logo is the same for different group types, and whether there will be misunderstood or generate antipathy. Universality may be the most complicated point, which requires certain amount of cultural accumulation in different countries. In the process of brand communication, different groups of people will be exposed to the logo. For multinational companies, cultural taboos in various regions also need to be taken into consideration. Therefore, many multinational companies will adopt relatively simple design methods, such as text Logos, to eliminate unnecessary associations or misunderstandings.

(6) Foresight

Foresight can also be understood as whether it is easily obsoletes. Classic and eternity are what every enterprise and designers aspire to. Therefore, when you are thinking, it is important not to blindly follow the so-called popular elements and styles, or an overnight success design methodology. The essence of design can be learned from reading more classical cases.

(7) Succinctness

Paul Rand proposed the question that whether designers need further consideration about the succinctness when the above six principles have been met.

Actually, Logo is used to replace text, therefore, a Logo only seeks for precision, splendid and texture without succinctness and quality is unlikely to survive. However, succinctness does not equal to simplicity. It means to remove all unnecessary redundant elements while retaining the uniqueness and recognition of the Logo, so that the main object could be highlighted. To be more specific, do not stroke the Logo or use too many colours and fonts styles. The overusage of gradients should be avoided.

Most people misunderstand Logo design as an "commentator", hoping to convey all content (and those related to the company) through the design. It is unnecessary to make the readers understand the company's business, products, services, ideas, etc. as soon as they see the Logo. Logo is just a simple symbol that cannot act as a guide. For example, the Nike Logo does not convey any information about Nike. But you can associate the Logo with Nike every time you see it.

Throughout the development history of design, subtraction is an eternal theme and designers continues to pursue recognizability whether it be architecture, interior design or graphic design. Many brands will abandon graphic elements, or flatten them from three-dimensional effects, or drop one language for those bilingual Logos.

When Logo design is evolving to the direction of becoming flat and succinct, the contradiction between "recognition" and "uniqueness" is revealed. On the one hand, we want the Logo to be succinct and clear, but we also hope it to be unique. Therefore, it is necessary to balance between the two aspects when designing. The memorability will decline if the recognizability is compromised in pursuit of uniqueness.

From the view of marketing, Logo design is all about perception and focuses on the transmission of feelings. There is no need to constantly impose visual elements in order to inform consumers what the brand is. Moreover, the complexity of graphics cannot reflect the ability of a designer because it takes the audience more time to think about what the brand name is, bring unpleasant experience.

4 The General Process of Logo Design

The general design process has the following three points:
A. Identify the problems and understand the requirements
B. Look for references and create Logo ideas
C. Draw sketches and render visualised presentation

4.1 Identify the problems and understand the requirements

The purpose of design is to solve the problem existed, and Logo design is no exception. Experienced designers often emphasize the importance of communication, because that only in the directions, can we improve the design efficiency and avoid useless efforts.

Sometimes, however, the customer's needs may be just a few lines, describing generally, such as "I want it to be high-end and generous", "I want it to be as simple as the Logo of Apple" or simply "you can give it a shot first". In fact, communications like these have a serious effect on the subsequent progress.

In these occasions, you need to dig into their implicit needs with your professional knowledge, helping them disassemble the purpose of designing the Logo step by step. For example, you may ask them, "What kind of vision do you want the Logo to convey?" or "Who are the target user group of your products?", to name but a few. The process of analysis reflects what you are thinking about, helping you to sort out the information and confirm direction. By interpreting and comprehending the information, you can make a breakthrough.

In this case, experienced designers will prepare a requirement form, used for analysing the problem together with the clients.

(1) The Chinese and English names and sources of the brand

In general, the Chinese and English names of the brand are the most basic elements in the Logo. After all, when the brand "recognition" is emphasized, we shall know the Logo before understanding it. Getting to know the sources of the brand helps to analyse the style of the brand and choose suitable fonts, colours, and design scheme.

(2) The products or services of the company

For companies with a clear product, the product is the best way to interpret the brand. For example, a brand that sells tea, wine or coffee can use the image of these goods in the graphic part of the Logo.

Designer: Yukihiko Aizawa

Design Agency: Henriquez Lara Estudio

When depicting a relatively abstract concept, we can make a subjective connection to build a visual image, by decorating the Logo name with some figurative techniques. For example, the core vision of Wonderlet is the firebird in Russian fairy tales. Inspired by the initial letter "W", the designer depicts a flying bird, creating a more deeply rooted brand image.

Design Agency: Funky Press

(3) Target users, leading brands and competing products in the industry

Even for the same type of brand, the style can vary greatly depending on the target audiences. Collect and sort out common Logos in the industry, summarise the tonality of the industry, clarify common elements, allows designers to understand the overall style and design trends of the industry.

(4) Styles that impress consumers

There are three general aesthetic styles: the style that the client likes, the style that meets industry standards, and the style that best reflects the designer's vision. The designer needs to make trade-offs and blend these three styles. The designers should get to know customers' preferences and their expectations for the Logo in advance, for instance, "a text-based Logo or a graphic-text-combined one?", "Logo dominated in Chinese or English, or a combined one?", "what colours do costumers prefer?" All these factors will affect the choice and typography of the Logo.

Questionnaire
1. What is the Chinese and English name of the brand and the implied meanings?
2. Does the brand have slogan or not? If so, what is it?
3. What products does the company sell? Or what service does it provide?
4. What is the brand positioning, or who are the target users?
5. The brand that the Logo design needs to refer to.
6. Favorite style.
7. Unacceptable style.
8. What are the specific requirements for the Logo design? For example: colour, shape, acronym, all capital letters, all lowercase letters, etc.
9. Taboos and other requirements.

4.2 Look for references and create Logo ideas

After understanding the needs of customers, don't rush to design. Brainstorm first, and write all related words on a piece of paper, then analyse them step by step. Select keywords, based on which searching for relevant elements, and record useful references. On this basis, disperse thinking, list the ideas you can think of so that you can choose among them.

Take the Babyface handmade dessert as an example. The client want the Logo to show "European style, classic, eternity and stylish sophistication". You can do an exercise first, list the keywords or objects you think that are suitable according to the method shown below, and then make choices according to the actual situation.

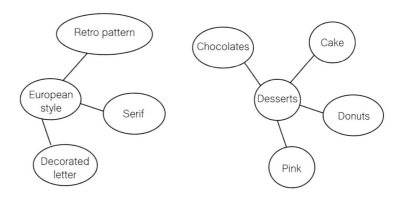

4.3 Draw sketches and render visualized presentation

Drawing sketches is the third step. You need to arrange and combine the selected keywords and elements creatively. At this stage, you can refer to the successful cases of other designers, and keep thinking and trying. At the same time, it is necessary to maintaining communication with client.

When you outline your sketch on papers, think about these questions: what symbol would be used to replace those texts? What font should you choose? How do different elements combine? How can images and texts be arranged? All these need to be resolved at the sketching stage.

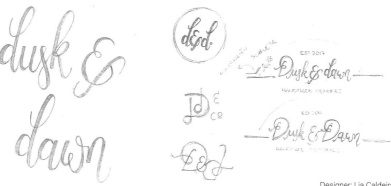

Designer: Lia Caldeira

If you are not sure about where to start, you might begin by imitating other cases and analysing the structure of the Logo, the changing at the end of the font, and the combination of elements. Apart from what you have designed, do you have any other ideas? Try drawing them out with your pencil and sorting out the reasons for this arrangement.

If possible, try to output more design cases that beyond clients' expectations in the draft stage, so as to provide them with more diverse choices. It is up to them to choose the suitable case, then you need to modify the selected one, and finish the design step by step.

Photo by Philipp Mandler on Unsplash

Back to the case of Babyface handmade dessert, 2tigers design studio has summarised the required visual elements as follows: Babyface brand name, bluebird, garden, decorative frame and lines. The initial drafts of the design endow the brand a European style, highlighting classic, eternity and fashion, as well as a unique sense of sophistication.

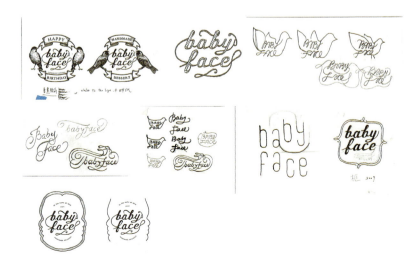

The bluebird alone has multiple options. The garden is represented by a variety of plants, including aloe vera flowers, ferns, pine and cypress leaves, with neutral-style to show a classic and austere personality.

Design Agency: 2tigers Design Studio

Since the client is in the wedding industry, it was finally decided to remain the bluebird, a symbol of happiness, with a retro European frame.

Design Agency: 2tigers Design Studio

In the sketch stage, three or four hours is recommended to stimulate your imagination and to draw 40~50 different Logos. Once you are immersed in it, there will be more in-depth research. By continuous experimentation, new inspirations will burst out.

The success of every project is born from the constant revision process. Therefore, you need to be fully committed and keep the original intention of the design in your mind at all times.

Chapter 2

FONT DESIGN IN LOGO

1 The Category of Fonts

Typeface refers to a complete set of text styles, such as Arial, Times New Roman, or Microsoft YaHei, AlibabaSans. Each font has its unique characteristics, which are embodied in each font.

Font is a more specific form of text style, which can be used in practice, involving the weight, size and width of the font. For example, Microsoft YaHei, bold, 12 pt is one font; Microsoft YaHei, extra thin, 8 pt is another font.

Glyph refers to the appearance and writing method of a single character. There must be differences between various text styles of the same English character or Chinese character. Therefore, in font design, designers can observe different glyphs of the same font, analyze the structure of the text and extract the design points.

Fonts play an important role in brand design and are closely related to graphics. Fonts to graphics is like green leaves to red flowers. Red flowers cannot be bright without green leaves as the foil. Of course, sometimes the font itself is the red flower.

1.1 Basic Styles and Structure of Chinese Characters

1.1.1 Basic styles of Chinese characters

The common text style of Chinese characters can be roughly divided into two categories: printed and calligraphic. The printed style includes SimSun and SimHei, while the calligraphy style includes regular script, cursive script, running script, official script and seal script[1].

(1) Printed style

SimSun is a Chinese character font designed for printing. It is characterized by thin horizontal strokes and thick vertical strokes, and clear edges and corners, with decorations called "Lin" at two ends of the stroke. In modern printing, it is mainly used for the main body of books, periodicals or newspapers. Because of the characteristics of thin horizontal and thick vertical, it is not prominent enough for headlines compared with SimHei. However, if the text of the whole poster is mainly in slim SimSun, it can also be used as the title font in order to maintain the unity of the layout.

Source Han Serif

[1] seal script will not be further discussed due to the low utilisation rate.

Mei-Ling Font

SimHei for Chinese characters was created according to the Western Sans-Serif after the introduction of modern printing. Its horizontal and vertical strokes are the same thickness, and the starting and ending strokes are square. SimHei is strong and thick, so it is very suitable for emphasizing the title, and it is also very clear after zooming in. However, because the Zihuai of SimHei is smaller than that of SimSun in the same size, it is not convenient for reading. So it is not suitable for text arrangement in small sizes. But due to the thick strokes and smaller Zihuai, it leaves people with the impression of introverted and calm, solemn and powerful, simple and generous. Geometric features are full of modern sense, which is also the basic font of many brand logo deformation.

YouYuan is a variant of SimHei, whose strokes are slender and easy to read. The turning point of strokes is more round and delicate, which is suitable for children books or products. For example, Youshe HaoShenTi is usually used.

Source Han Sans

Youshe HaoShenTi

(2) Calligraphy

Calligraphy is a unique artistic form to show the beauty of characters in China. On the basis of information record and transfer, it expresses its graceful shape and exquisite meaning. The common calligraphic styles are clerical, regular, cursive and running script.

Clerical script, developed from seal script, turns circle into square and arc into straight. The structure is slightly wide and flat, with long rightward stroke and short downward stroke, in a solemn style. In addition, it focus on starting magnificently and ending lightly, full of twists and turns.

Part of *Caoquanbei*

Regular script, evolved from official script, is a modern handwriting style for Chinese character with a square shape and straight strokes.

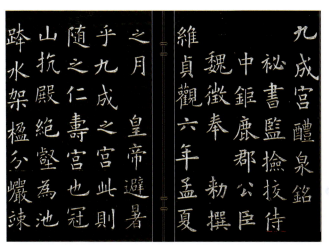

Part of Ouyang Xun's *Jiuchenggongliquanming*

Cursive script originated from the scribbled clerical script, including three categories which are Zhangcao, Jincao and Kuangcao. Cursive script generally simplifies the official handwriting and looks obscurely, so it is not suitable for long articles.

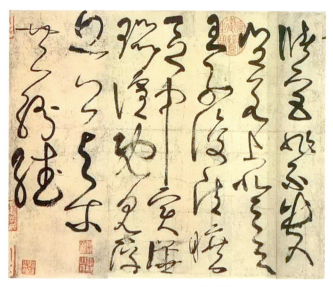

Part of Zhang Xu's *Four Ancient Posts*

Running script originated from official script, including Xingkai and Xingcao. Compared with cursive script, it is easier to read because it is less simplified, less linked and less slanted. Due to the writing characteristics of cursive and running script, they are more suitable for vertical typesetting, showing elegant classical charm. It can be used as a decorative element in posters.

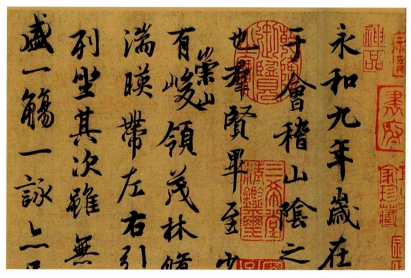

Part of Wang Xizhi's *Lantingxu*

1.1.2 Basic structure of Chinese characters

Before designing a font, we should fully understand the structure of the font and choose the appropriate deformation method according to the structure or stroke trend of the font.

(1) Skeleton of Chinese characters (The form of Chinese characters)

Chinese characters are composed of various specific points and lines. From general to specific, they are divided into four levels: characters, components, strokes and shapes. As shown in the figure below, take " 湖 " (which means lake in English) as an example. The designer can redesign the strokes according to the creative concept and structural characteristics of the font, but pay attention to the integrity between the components.

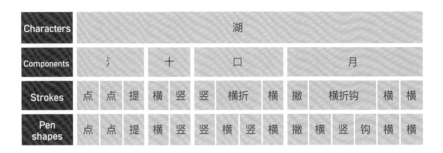

Characters	湖											
Components	氵			十			口		月			
Strokes	点	点	提	横	竖	竖	横折	横	撇	横折钩	横	横
Pen shapes	点	点	提	横	竖	竖	横	竖	横	撇	横	竖	钩	横	横

Different characters have different stroke numbers. According to the components of Chinese characters, they can be divided into one-component characters and combined characters. A one-component character has only one component, also known as a single structure; while a combined character has multiple components and can be roughly divided into seven structures.

1. ⬜ (Left and right structure)

2. ⬜ (Upper and lower structure)

3. ⬜ (Left, middle and right structure)

4. ⬜ (Upper, middle and lower structure)

5. Semi-surrounded structure：

(1) . ⬜ (Upper right surrounded structure)

(2) . ⬜ (Upper left surrounded structure)

(3) . ⬜ (Lower left surrounded structure)

(4) . ⬜ (Upper three quarters surrounded structure)

(5) . ⬜ (Lower three quarters surrounded structure)

(6) . ⬜ (Left three quarters surrounded structure)

6. 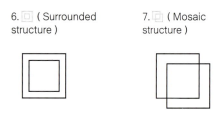 (Surrounded structure)

7. (Mosaic structure)

(2) Five dimensions affecting Chinese characters

The basic attributes of Chinese characters

01 Zimian   02 Core   03 Weight   04 Zhonggong   05 Zihuai

① Zimian and Zishen

Before designing Chinese font (as well as Japanese and Korean, etc.), clarify the two "boxes" of each font. One is the large outer box called the "Zishen box" (the illusion itself), and the other is the small inner box called the "Zimian box" (the benchmark box), which is the actual area of the font itself.

面 —— Zishen box
  —— Zimian box

身 —— Zishen box
  —— Zimian box

When the font size is the same, the font with larger Zimian looks larger and makes the complete text compact. On the contrary, the font with smaller Zimian looks smaller, with wider space between each character, and the complete text looks more open.

All of the above are 36 pt fonts

However, due to the features of Chinese characters, not every word will support the whole Zimian box. Some words are flat (such as " 一 "and " 工 ") and some are slender (such as " 月 " and " 目 "). However, when designing fonts, try to layout the font in the Zimian box, so that each word will appear unified and natural after combined.

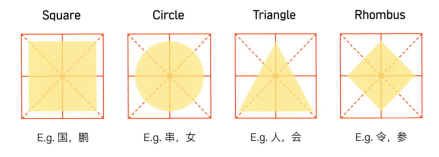

Square	Circle	Triangle	Rhombus
E.g. 国，鹏	E.g. 串，女	E.g. 人，会	E.g. 令，参

Fonts with various shapes and areas have various Zimian visually

② Centre and core

The centre refers to the geometric centre point of the font's frame, which is an actual point, not the centre of the font. The core is the visual centre of the font, which is usually slightly higher than the centre. It is the weight centre of the font. The centre is often used to adjust the position of the core. When designing fonts, you need to consider the weight and actuality of the font, determine the position of its core, and ensure the harmony between characters.

Because people's visual centre is generally upward, the core of standard fonts is generally upper than the centre while fonts with a lower core looks more stable.

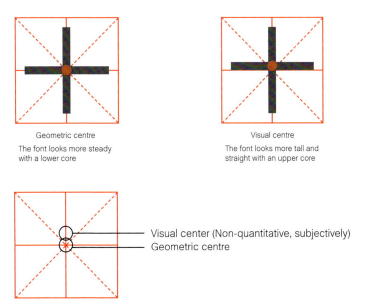

Geometric centre
The font looks more steady with a lower core

Visual centre
The font looks more tall and straight with an upper core

Visual center (Non-quantitative, subjectively)
Geometric centre

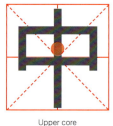

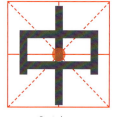

| Upper core | Central core | Lower core |

The font with an upper core and a slender shape generally shows elegance and is suitable for delicate products that are for the young, females or emphasize quality.

③ Weight

Weight refers to the thickness degree of the same font. According to the different usage of fonts, 4 to 7 fonts of different thickness are usually designed. Some fonts even have more than 10 varieties of different thickness.

For example, the commercially free font, Alibaba Sans, has 5 kinds of weight, which are Light, Regular, Medium, Bold, and Heavy.

阿里巴巴普惠体 Light

阿里巴巴普惠体 Regular

阿里巴巴普惠体 **Medium**

阿里巴巴普惠体 **Bold**

阿里巴巴普惠体 **Heavy**

Another common font, Source Han Sans, has 7 kinds of weight, which are Extra Light, Light, Normal, Regular, Medium, Bold, and Heavy.

思源黑体 ExtraLight

思源黑体 Light

思源黑体 Normal

思源黑体 Regular

思源黑体 Medium

思源黑体 Bold

思源黑体 Heavy

The comparison shows that the thinness of Alibaba Sans and the extreme thinness of Source Han Sans look similar. Therefore, the standard of weight is relative, and the weight of different fonts is not comparable.

The font with one kind of weight can not perfectly meet different situations, while various kinds of weight can enhance the practicability of the font and can be applied to titles, paragraphs or posters.

Although the bold font can also achieve the effect of font thickening, it just makes the text conspicuous and will affect the structure and beauty of the font. Its visual effect is not as good as that of changing weight of the font.

Standard effect: 字体在品牌设计中运用

Increase weight: **字体在品牌设计中运用**

Bolded effect: **字体在品牌设计中运用**

④ Zhonggong

The concept of Zhonggong comes from calligraphy and refers to the central space of Chinese characters. When copying calligraphy, a boundary lattice is used to aid the practice, commonly known as Matts, Mizi grid (looks like the Union Flag) and Nine-box. The centre of the Nine-box is Zhonggong. In short, Zhonggong is the area around the core of Chinese characters.

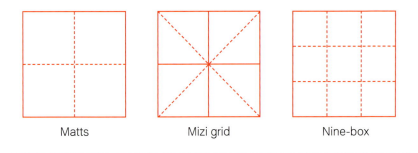

| Matts | Mizi grid | Nine-box |

Boundary lattices generally used in calligraphy

Zhonggong mainly has two varieties, which are the tight Zhonggong and the loose Zhonggong. They affect the tightness of the font structure, the size of Zimian and the height of the font's core.

Tight Zhonggong: the font strokes gather together or close to the Zhonggong box. It looks tight inside and loose outside, with a smaller Zimian.

Loose Zhonggong: the font is scattered or the strokes are far away from the Zhonggong box. It looks tight outside and loose inside, with a larger Zimian.

If the Zhonggong is too large, it is not suitable for text typesetting. Because it looks loose and not compact, which will affect the reading experience and making people unable to concentrate.

Tight Zhonggong

Zhonggong

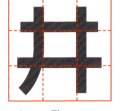

Loose Zhonggong

Source Han Sans

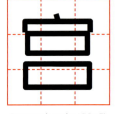

Pangmenzhengdao XiXianTi

Source Han Sans has a tight Zhonggong structure.

Pangmenzhengdao XiXianTi has a loose Zhonggong structure.

⑤ Zihuai and Zigu

The concept of Zihuai is often found in books related to Japanese font design, which refers to the left blank part in the font. The weight of characters will affect the Zihuai size, so you can never design a thick bold font with thick strokes but large Zihuai.

Zihuai refers to the left blank part between strokes

Zigu also known as Counter in English. The concept of Zigu comes from Western letters, which refers to the partially or completely enclosed space in letters. The bigger Zigu is, the easier the font can be recognized.

Although Zihuai and Zigu have different origins and names, their meanings are roughly the same. (For the convenience of understanding and distinguishing, Zihuai is used to analyze Chinese characters while Zigu is used for English.)

Zigu refers to a partially or completely enclosed space in letters

Font design should not only pay attention to black characters, but also pay attention to the white space inside and between fonts. "White" here refers to the negative form in the positive and negative forms. No matter Chinese characters, English letters or images, visual balance can be achieved only when the positive and negative forms are balanced.

In practice, designers need to pay attention to the relationship between the size of the Zihuai or Zigu. For example, the upper and lower Zigu of the letter "B" are designed exactly the same. According to the principle of visual illusion, the upper Zigu will appear larger, making the whole font look shaky. If you make the upper Zigu smaller while the lower bigger, the whole letter looks very stable and more balanced.

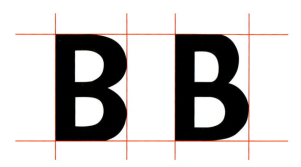

The positive and negative forms are also related to the text spacing, which determines the rhythm of the article, affecting reading experience. Therefore, when designing black characters, the shape and proportion of white space should be considered at the same time, such as the white space at the turning point of the letter "r".

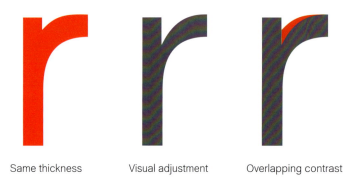

| Same thickness | Visual adjustment | Overlapping contrast |

1.2 Basic Styles and Structure of English Letters

1.2.1 Basic styles of English fonts

English fonts can be roughly divided into two types: Serif and Sans Serif, corresponding to SimSun and SimHei in Chinese fonts respectively. Besides, there are other fonts, such as Gothic, Script, Display, etc.

(1) Serif

Serif refers to the font with serif, which is the decorative detail at the end of the font stroke. The horizontal stroke of serif is thin and the vertical stroke is thick, which is similar to SimSun.

Because of the decoration of serif, the beginning and end of strokes are emphasized, which makes it easily recognized and suitable for text typesetting. Besides, with high readability, it also decreases the possibility of reading the wrong line.

In Europe, serif is usually used to show the "advanced", "traditional", "classical" and "steady" style, but we cannot just say that "serif = advanced". In the continuous development of serif, some varieties of serif become to emphasize fashion and modernity, and even reflects the trend of the combination of retro and modern.

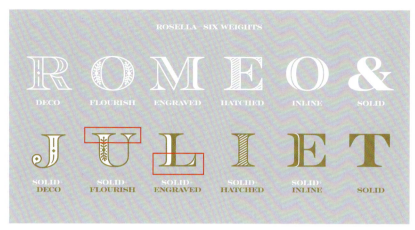

Monotype Imaging: Rosella™ Typeface

Drizy Studio: Andimia

According to the historical development order, the main styles of serif can be roughly divided into five types: Humanist, Old style, Transitional, Modern, and Slab serif.

Humanistic: Jenson, Kennerley, Centaur, Stempel Schneidler, Verona, Lutetia

Old style: Adobe Jenson, Janson, Garamond, Bembo, Goudy Old Style

Transitional: Times Roman, Baskerville

Modern: Didot, Bodoni, Century, Computer Modern

Slab serif: Rockwell, Courier, Clarendon

Serif comparison of five fonts

① Humanistic

Humanistic fonts, which emerged in the 1560s, are also known as Venetian fonts because of their popularity in Italy. The font is based on the handwritten fonts of Italian humanist writers, and retains many characteristics of handwriting: the horizontal stroke in the middle of "e" leans to the upper right, the x-height is relatively low, and the thickness of the strokes barely changes.

Jenson

Centaur

Stempel Schneidler

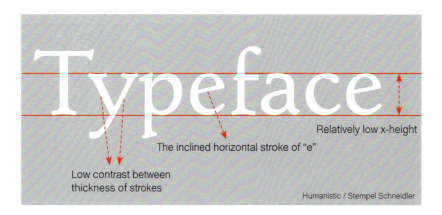

Relatively low x-height

The inclined horizontal stroke of "e"

Low contrast between thickness of strokes

Humanistic / Stempel Schneidler

② Old style

Compared with Humanistic fonts, Old style fonts have removed many characteristics of handwriting and are more delicate. The thickness of strokes no longer stays at a uniform width but have contrast. The x-height is also higher and the axis inclines more, with an arc-shaped serif and gentler transition at the intersection of the strokes. The thinnest part of the letter appears on slanted strokes, not vertical or horizontal strokes. The style is traditional and gentle, and is often used for typesetting of the content in books, newspapers and magazines.

Adobe Jenson Pro

Garamond

Goudy Old Style

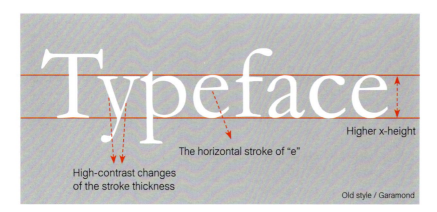

Higher x-height

The horizontal stroke of "e"

High-contrast changes of the stroke thickness

Old style / Garamond

③ Transitional

The Transitional fonts almost completely abandon the characteristics of handwriting, with more contrasting line thicknesses and more smooth serif curves, which are more noticeable than Old style fonts, but not as good as Modern fonts. Because the thin strokes are too thin, the Transitional font is not suitable for text part. Generally, it is used in titles or logos because there is enough space to display its smooth curves.

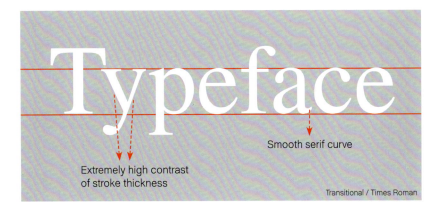

Smooth serif curve

Extremely high contrast of stroke thickness

Transitional / Times Roman

④ Modern

Modern fonts are recognized as the most beautiful and stylish fonts in English fonts. Some fashion and luxury brands will use modern fonts as brand fonts. Modern fonts have developed the thickness contrast of Transitional fonts to the extreme. The serifs are getting sharper, the angles are closer to vertical, and x-height is getting higher and higher.

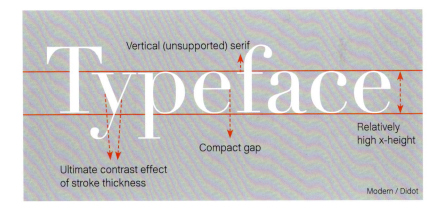

Vertical (unsupported) serif

Relatively high x-height

Compact gap

Ultimate contrast effect of stroke thickness

Modern / Didot

⑤ Slab Serif

Slab Serif fonts are characterized by thick quadrangular serifs. The thickness of the serifs is similar to that of strokes, and there is almost no contrast of stroke thickness. It is not only classical like serifs but also modern and fashion, which is suitable for the retro fashion brands.

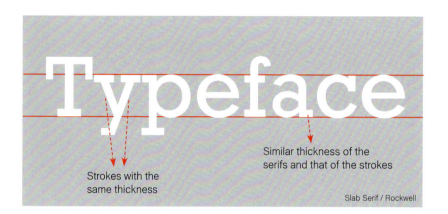

Strokes with the same thickness

Similar thickness of the serifs and that of the strokes

Slab Serif / Rockwell

By comparing Old style fonts with Modern fonts, we can see that throughout the development of serifs, the contrast between horizontal and vertical strokes has become stronger and stronger, and the style of serifs has become more and more sharp.

Diagonal emphasis line
Slanted, bracketed serifs

Softer thickness transitions

Old style

Garamond
Palatino

Vertical emphasis line
Horizontal, extremely thin serifs

Strong contrast of thickness

Modern

Didot
Bodoni

According to the comparison above, we can summarize some tips that are suitable for serif changes and can be used in our own font design.

· The inclination angle of the axis: left-inclined to vertical.
· Thickness contrast of strokes: becoming more and more obvious.
· The inclination angle of serifs: the angle between the strokes tends to be right angle.

Various serif types:

(2) Sans Serif

Sans Serif is similar to SimHei of Chinese characters. It completely abandons the decorative serifs. It looks simple and the stroke thickness contrast is weak, which is more modern. It is said that this type of font was designed for titles. If the font size is reduced for content typesetting, it will greatly affect the reading effect.

Sans Serif can be subdivided into four categories: Grotesque, Neo-Grotesque, Geometric, and Humanist.

Grotesque: Grotesque, Royal Gothic, Franklin Gothic
Neo-Grotesque: Helvetica, Arial, Univers
Geometric: vant Garde, Century Gothic, Futura, Gotham
Humanist: Verdana, Optima, Frutiger, Segeo

Four kinds of Sans Serif

① Grotesque

Akzidenz-Grotesk, the most popular early Grotesque, originated in the late nineteenth century and was used exclusively in print for commercial campaigns, such as advertisements, tickets and forms. Because it did not match the aesthetics of the time, it was once considered an ugly and strange font.

Franklin Gothic BT

Akzidenz-Grotesk

Grotesque MT

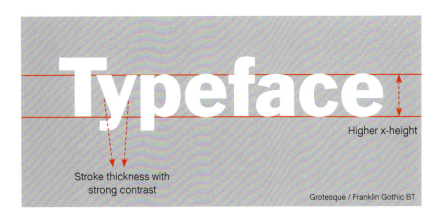

Higher x-height

Stroke thickness with strong contrast

Grotesque / Franklin Gothic BT

② Neo-Grotesque

Neo-Grotesque is now known as the standard Sans Serif font, represented by the well-known Helvetica, which has been at the top of the bestseller lists since its release.

The design of Helvetica follows the modernism idea, emphasizes functionality rather than decoration, pays attention to the recognition and readability of fonts, and highlights information transferring function of fonts. It focuses on the font itself. The concise design makes it easier to express user's idea accurately.

Its main feature, neutrality, allows it to be used in various scenes.

Neo-Grotesque

Helvetica Neue

Arial

Univers

Flat top

Horizontal

Vertical

Helvetica Neue

Futura Bk Bt
Century Gothic
Gotham

③ Geometric

The Geometric font is based on geometric structure, expressing the beauty of geometry through the sharp contrast of straight lines and arcs. For example, Paul Renner created Futura inspired by the Bauhaus movement. The shape is well-designed, dominated by horizontal and vertical hard strokes.

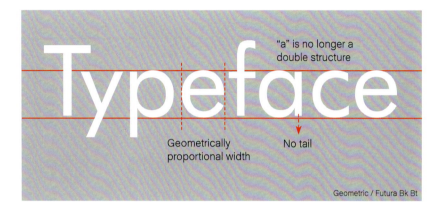

"a" is no longer a double structure

Geometrically proportional width

No tail

Geometric / Futura Bk Bt

In contrast to the representation of Neo-Grotesque, Helvetica, "A" and "V" in Futura have sharp tops and bottoms, and rounded letters are more rounded. The ascending part and descending part are longer, and the width of "E" and "F" is narrower, mainly slender. "G", "O", and "Q" are in perfect circles. This font is commonly used in products and brands with a sense of design, such as LV and OMEGA.

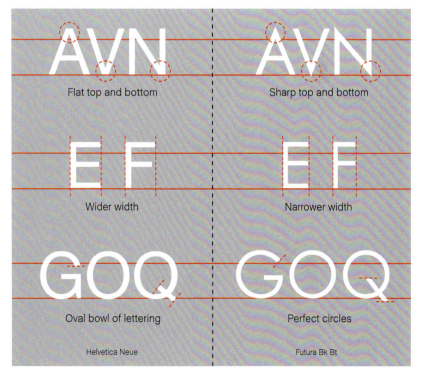

Flat top and bottom

Sharp top and bottom

Wider width

Narrower width

Oval bowl of lettering

Perfect circles

Helvetica Neue

Futura Bk Bt

④ Humanist

The humanist font draws on the proportion and structure of classical fonts, presenting a better sense of rhythm. It is more elegant than Helvetica and has a more calligraphic style. It is the most humanistic font in Sans Serif. It is represented by Myriad, Gill Sans, Frutiger, Tahoma, Verdana, Optima, and Lucide Grande, etc. Its x-height of is relatively small; the ending of letters such as "e" and "s" adopts a semi-enclosed structure, which is more open.

Humanist

Myriad Pro
Gill Sans Std
Verdana

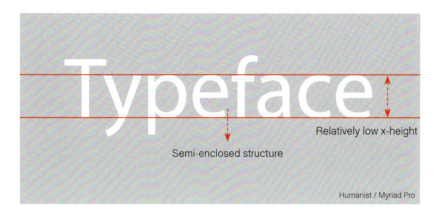

Relatively low x-height

Semi-enclosed structure

Humanist / Myriad Pro

(3) Other fonts

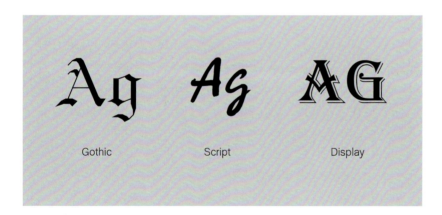

Gothic   Script   Display

① Gothic

Gothic font is written with a flat-tipped pen. The wide stroke is generally at an angle of 35 to 40 degrees from the horizontal. Gothic font is gorgeous and highly decorative, and it pays attention to the bending of lines and changes in thickness.

Designer: Vedran Vaskovic

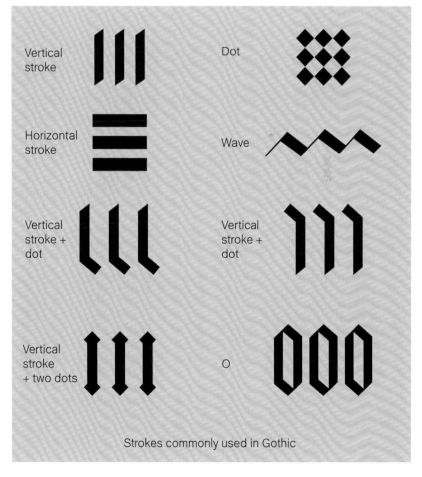

Vertical stroke	Dot
Horizontal stroke	Wave
Vertical stroke + dot	Vertical stroke + dot
Vertical stroke + two dots	O

Strokes commonly used in Gothic

② Handwriting

The styles of handwriting are more varied, such as Italic and Display penmanship. There are elegant and classical fonts, as well as title fonts with thick strokes. When using handwriting, you need to avoid using all uppercase fonts, which easily affects readability. In addition, too much handwriting fonts will make the entire layout look cluttered. Generally, you can enlarge it for titles, or reduce its size for decoration.

Tiranti Solid LET

Designer: Jacklina Jekova

③ Display

Ornamental font endows the text with a unique style through exaggerated deformation. For example, Decoracha Font, designed by høly, adds more decorative variation to letters by lengthening their extensions and descends.

høly™: Decoracha Font

The Telka font designed by Kristina Selinski uses circle as the main element in each letter, which is the reference for stroke design, creating a strong sense of decoration.

Designer: Kristina Selinski

Paul Bokslag designed the letters in a three-dimensional style, using negative space to represent the letters.

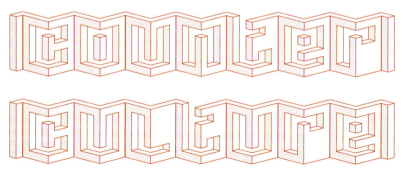

Designer: Paul Bokslag

1.2.2 Basic structure of English letters

Just like how we talk about Chinese characters, this chapter will introduce each part of English letters in detail just to help you fully understand the basic structure and broaden design ideas.

Bodoni

Baseline: The baseline is used when multiple letters are arranged. As shown in the figure below, the lowercase letters in English have the concept of "ascender" and "descender". They need to be arranged with the central core part as the axis, and the red line below is the baseline for the arrangement of letters.

Mean line: Height line of lowercase letters without ascending parts.

x-height: X-height refers to the distance between the baseline and the mean line. It is also the height of the lowercase letter "x". x-height is not fixed. When it is higher, the entire font will look larger. How high should it be? How long should the ascender and descender be? The proportion, the style and the use of the font are closely related to the setting of these values.

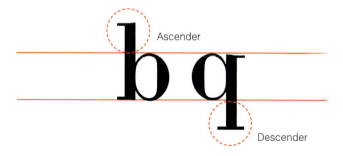

Bodoni

Ascender: The part where "h" and "b" extend upward beyond the mean line.

Descender: The part where "p" and "q" extend downward beyond the baseline.

Ascender and descender increase the recognition of words, especially for readers whose native language is not English, lowercase will be easier to identify than uppercase for the same word.

Because East Asian characters (Chinese, Japanese, etc.) do not have a baseline, when East Asian fonts are used with Western fonts, the bottom of East Asian characters should be aligned with the baseline.

Stem   Arm   Bowl

Bodoni

Stem: The main strokes of a letter. Usually it is the vertical strokes, sometimes it refers to the slanted strokes.

Arm: The horizontal strokes of the letter.

Bowl: The part where the strokes are curved.

Counter: The inner space formed by the stem and the bowl of a letter, whether it is closed or not.

Word Hole   Terminal   Wordline

Bodoni

Word Hole: The opening at the bottom of the letter.

Terminal: The decorative part of the letter.

Wordline: The thinnest part of a serif body.

Tail   Tip   Shoulder

Bodoni

Tail: Decorative descending stroke, which can be found in capital "R".

Tip: A stroke that tapers at the end.

Shoulder: The curved part that extends from the stem.

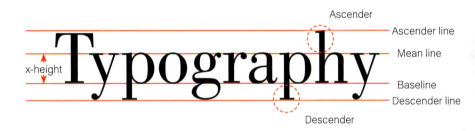

Ascender

Ascender line

Mean line

x-height

Baseline

Descender line

Descender

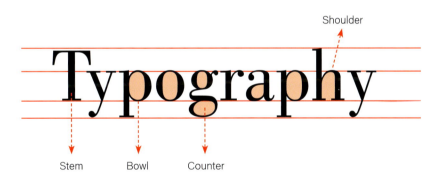

Shoulder

Stem   Bowl   Counter

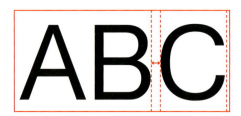

Tracking: Tracking has different meanings for font designers and font users. Font designer needs to ensure that there is blank on the left and right side of each letter to make it easier to read. For font users, tracking refers to the adjustment of letter space after the font is arranged into words.

Kerning: It refers to the space between specific letter combinations. It is the readjustment of word space for combinations of different letters on the basis of the standard word space. Because different letters have different shapes, if all letters are uniformly spaced, the whole word will be inharmonious.

For example, there is a standard word space between "T" and "H", but when "A" and "V" is grouped together, due to the shape of the two letters, their positions can overlap. If the kerning is not adjusted in a targeted manner, it will look alienated.

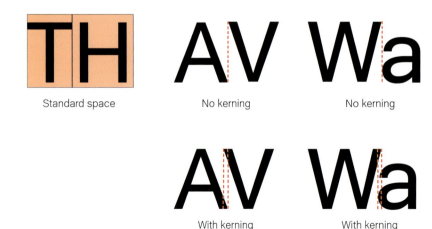

Standard space   No kerning   No kerning

With kerning   With kerning

2 Application Scenarios of Fonts

2.1 Logo, Slogan and Descriptive Text

There are three main applications of fonts in brand design, namely logo, slogan, and descriptive text.

2.1.1 Logo

In brand design, the importance of the font logo is the same as that of the graphic logo. A good font design can be recognizable and impressive. In most cases, in order to maintain the brand uniqueness, designers need to design fonts for the logo to avoid the similarity with the words used by other brands.

Different fonts convey different emotions. Fonts with thick strokes make people feel strong and powerful, while fonts with thin strokes appear light and flexible. Chapter 2.1 introduces a lot of font classifications, and the following is a specific analysis of their use in real cases.

① SimSun / Serif

The slender lines of SimSun and Serif make them more feminine and suitable for conveying a classical, formal, and delicate tone, so the logo based on the serif is deeply loved by the fashion industry. For example, the logos and titles of brands or magazines such as Dior, Harper's Bazaar, and VOGUE, all take serif Didot[1] as their standard font. Didot retains the classic beauty of traditional serifs while delivering the modern style with sharp corners. Therefore, the Serif represented by Didot has gradually become a stylish, elegant and modern exclusive font.

Didot

ABCDEFGHIJKLMNOPQRSTUVWXYZ
abcdefghijklmnopqrstuvwxyz1234567890

---

[1] Developed from 1784 to 1811, Didot is named after a famous French family who made great contributions to publishing, printing and font design.

La Pinta Puro Ibérico de Bellota is a company whose main products are sausage and ham. Designer chooses Serif as the logo font, presenting the cultural tradition and high quality of the product with a both modern and historical visual image. The logo conveys a sense of high-class through the font.

Design Agency: Bullseye

The font logo of Qingyao Xinpai casserole fish tends to be young, soft and flat. The horizontal strokes of the Chinese font try to present a light ending stroke like water droplets. On the basis of font recognition, the pinyin "QingYao" is added to the printed version in concert with the Chinese characters, which improves the texture and balance. Thus, its unique font temperament is created. Because the main logo font has a lot of deformations, the subtitle is not advised to be too complicated. It's better to choose Serif which is more recognizable and can distinguish the priority of the titles.

Perfect Design: Qingyao Xinpai Casserole Fish

② SimHei / Sans Serif

SimHei and Sans Serif completely abandon the decorative serifs. Their structure is simple, the stroke thickness is basically the same, the presentation of a single font is emphasized, and the shape is concise and powerful. It has strong plasticity and can be easily modified in the later period. When there is no certain style, more styles can be generated later through the deformation of strokes.

The Chinese and English logos of V·Taste, as well as other necessary explanatory texts are selected in simple and clear Sans Serif fonts to convey the relaxing brand atmosphere, which is "smile and enjoyment". At the same time, it is also suitable for interesting deformation of young slang words such as "Cuibobo" (which means crisp) and "Xiangpenpen" (which means delicious) through Sans Serif.

Asia One Communications Group: V·Taste

Something More Near: Tonkotsu

③ Calligraphy / Handwriting

The characters " 盛京串道 " use the regular script of calligraphy style to emphasize its cultural features. The beginning and end of each character complement each other, maintaining the overall unity. In terms of corner mark, the use of curse gestures to enhance the brushstrokes of the word " 撸 " to breaks the single rhythm of the four characters. At the same time, the choice of English fonts also incorporates the style of calligraphy. The stroke style is between Serifs and Sans Serifs, making oriental charm diffuse.

Doyles chooses handwriting as the basic font of the logo, highlighting the brand's sense of history and quality, with a strong nostalgic atmosphere.

Perfect Design: Mukden Skewers

The Creative Method: Doyles Seafood

2.1.2 Slogan

The slogan of the brand is also inseparable from the font design. Slogan is a kind of external display of corporate brand image and the external presentation of brand positioning. A brand slogan usually expresses its service concept or promotes products in the form of a few words or a sentence.

Slogan embodies the personality, story, and values of the entire brand. At the same time, its function is to express the characteristics and advantages of enterprises or commodities in the shortest words, and condense them into one or two sentences of introduction.

The functions of slogans include expressing ideas, promoting interests, representing the brand, and narrowing the communication distance. Conveying brand emotion is the most important function of slogan. Slogan can also convey the company's product philosophy to consumers, emphasizing the most salient features of a company and its products. Often the most important brand strategy is in its slogan. And when it faces consumers, it presents only words. It is conceivable that fonts play an important role in slogan.

Tips for designing logo
Nowadays, many designers do post-drawing directly on the computer after drawing the sketch. It can be said that the overall operation is performed through the computer. The final draft is actually the product of focusing on the text for a long time, enlarging the part, and only focusing on the depiction of details. In this way, the overall structural relationship is often ignored, so that after the reduction, the overall presentation is not satisfactory. It will also cause subtle problems in the partial design of the logo, such as the unstable core of the font, or too many decorative elements destroy the overall effect, or some Zimian is large while some is small, or the stroke thickness is not well arranged, making the positive and negative spaces of the font not coordinated enough.
Therefore, in the final stage of font design, you can print fonts of different sizes on a piece of A3 paper to see the relationship between their different proportions in physical printing. You can also place it on the conference board to observe the structure, proportional space, stroke thickness, etc. of the font from a distance. In the process of observation, keep asking yourself a series of questions. For example, is the overall structure comfortable? Should the space between fonts be increased or decreased? Will the relationship of some strokes be clear if put them in the smallest proportion? In addition, don't blindly trust the results of the software, insist on printing the design, observe carefully, and believe what your eyes observe, find problems, and readjust until you are satisfied with the results.

In the brand design of SiuMai King, "市井美食，美味有迹可循" (which means you can find tasty food in the market) and "Street Flavor" are the slogans of the brand. The brand originated in the market of Brunei. After two generations of persistence, it has accumulated a certain local popularity. The slogan plays a role in expressing ideals and shortening the communication distance. In terms of font design selection, the combination of Chinese regular script and English handwriting has both the steadiness of Chinese and the playfulness of English.

Perfect Design: SiuMai King

The brand of SinYee Gongcha uses a large number of slogans. It is located in a fast-paced consumption area. A large number of consumers spend their time buying milk tea. Therefore, the main copy of the illustration is "delicious drinks don't need to tell stories", making milk tea instead of wasting time on explaining about raw materials and so on. The brand copy "understand your thoughts and give you a cup of love" is a conceptual breakdown of SinYee Gongcha, whose target consumers are females. In terms of design, all the text adopts the SimSun, which have similar characteristics with the Serif, conveying a sense of delicacy.

Copywriting for illustration elements

好 喝 的 饮 品 不 用 讲 故 事
MIND GONG CHA

Copywriting for the brand

懂 你 的 一 点 心 思　 给 你 的 一 杯 心 意 ①　　　重 要 的 是 你 的 心 意 ②
舌 尖 值 得 在 美 好 的 事 物 上 停 留 ③

Perfect Design: SinYee Gongcha

Xiao Guan Gao is a kind of health care products, and its slogan belongs to the category of expressing ideas to consumers. In the slogan design, it is not only text to display, but to match the overall tone of the brand, using graphic design elements as the carrier of slogan. This is to make the transition between logo and slogan more natural, and also to strengthen slogan.

Perfect Design: Xiao Guan Gao

The words " 优雅到老 " (which means keeping elegant all your life) represent the Tingfei's brand philosophy of perfection. It chooses the elegant Serif (SimSun), increases the word space between each character, and reduces the text at the same time. When it comes to the relationship with the logo, it moves backward to the second echelon of the overall design, without stealing the limelight of the logo.

Perfect Design: Tingfei

2.1.3 Descriptive text

Descriptive text generally refers to text other than logos and slogans, such as small print introductions on packaging or instructions for use, as well as menus of catering brands. As a supplementary copy, descriptive text is the main source for the audience to understand the brand. The main features are a wide range of use, a large application ratio, and a small font size. Generally, the same type of font as the logo and slogan is selected to maintain the overall unity.

In the design at this period, it is necessary to give priority to the legibility and recognition of the font, followed by the design sense of the font. If the overall proportion of the text is large, it is recommended to choose more common fonts such as SimSun and SimHei, and do not choose calligraphy, artistic fonts, etc., so as not to affect reading.

In the brand design of SiuMai King, the font of the business card is Sans Serif (SimHei), which is easy for reading, while the font of the menu is Serif, similar to the SimSun in its slogan, maintaining the unity of the overall layout.

Perfect Design: SiuMai King

Never ignore the font design for your brand and treat it like a graphic if you can. Design can't be empty talk. In addition to mastering the corresponding rules and techniques, it needs comprehension through continuous practice. In addition, you have to consider the visual characteristics of the text font, as well as the style collocation with other graphics, and integrate it into the overall brand composition.

Note: While using fonts, do not ignore copyright issues and respect the font developer's design copyright. If you do not have the budget to buy fonts, please choose fonts that are free for commercial use.

2.2 Auxiliary Graphics and Auxiliary Texts

In brand design, in addition to the graphic and font design in the logo, auxiliary graphics and auxiliary text have become more and more flexible and vivid. It is no longer the graphic display forms that simply revolves around the logo in the regular VI manual. More and more auxiliary graphics and text directly reflect the brand's interests and values through designing, including the use of geometric figures, the design of illustrations and the design of auxiliary fonts.

For novice designers, when designing such elements, two extremes are often prone to occur. One is that they do not know what to put in the content, and they cannot think of a good element style after brainstorms; the other is thinking too much. Too many complex elements listed distract consumers' attention, making consumers confused.

Therefore, good design of auxiliary fonts and graphics should start from customer's requirements of the brand, dig out the real core interests of the brand, and carry out divergent designs. In the design process, it is important to consider the relationship between these elements and the brand, as well as their priority, so as not to overwhelm it.

At the same time, good graphic design does not have to use graphics or text alone. Their combination is also a good idea. In the case of combined use, the style of graphics and fonts should be unified to avoid creating a sense of separation for consumers. Good graphic symbols and text must be in line with the overall image and temperament of the brand.

In the brand design of Macau Doulao by Perfect Design, a large number of fonts and graphics are used in the presentation, supplemented by interesting text, such as "Awesome", "Double-click on the 666", "Have a toast", "Likes", "You have not eaten yet", etc., to show the brand characteristics. At the same time, different colour matching and typography methods are used to stimulate different effects, so that the regional consumer groups can recognize and resonate, and achieve the relaxed and comfortable cultural atmosphere that the brand wants to convey.

The design of graphic symbols and text is inseparable from life. Find more details and beauty in life, put them into the design after processing, and you will definitely gain something.

 × ×

Perfect Design: Macao Doulao

3 Basic Font Design Techniques

3.1 Eight Steps of Yong

As an important rule of calligraphy entry, the Eight Steps of Yong has always been praised by people. It is respected because the shape of "Yong" is simple, the structure is square and neat. Although it has few strokes, it also contains many basic techniques of calligraphy without repetition. Therefore, if you master the Eight Steps of Yong, you will be able to do everything in the font structure and stroke application, and master the writing method of each character.

In the Standard of Modern Chinese, the character Yong has five strokes in total, but the dedicate font contains eight strokes, which are: Horizontal stroke, Vertical stroke, Left-falling stroke, Right-falling stroke, Raising stroke, Dot stroke, Turning stroke, Hook stroke. The picture below shows the eight kinds of strokes of Yong.

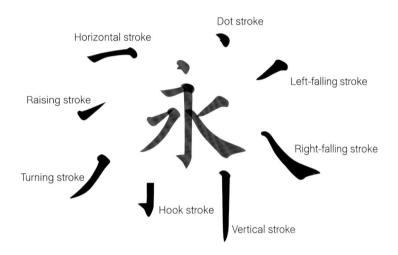

In font design, the brand name can be presented not only in a single character, but also by the superposition of several characters or Chinese words. When designing fonts, many novice designers will lack big-picture awareness. There will be various problems in the overall design. The common problems include the incongruity of fonts and the lack of integrity.

How to solve these problems step by step? We can adopt the ancient Eight Steps of Yong to complete a more unified font design. However, the principle is not to spell out the word "Yong", but to summarize the strokes of Yong. Design the strokes uniformly first, and then design the font.

Step 1. Design strokes

First of all, if the design lacks inspiration at the beginning, don't rush to make the first complete character, you can start from the strokes.

Many designers may be ready to design fonts in computer software immediately after they have conceived the inspiration on the sketch, but in fact, the plan at this time is not comprehensive and needs to be improved. Mindlessly operation can easily lead to design difficulties.

So at this time you need to perfect the sketch and design all the strokes of Yong. Once again, although the Eight Steps of Yong are related, it is not to simply make up a Yong, but to extract different radical strokes, and at the same time, you can also add other commonly used strokes. Continue to figure out and adjust the proportional relationship between each stroke, and design the ending form of the stroke (you can refer to p059 "Deformation of a Single Stroke"). Although you haven't done any word design at this stage, you have completed 50% of the design actually.

Taking Xiao Guan Gao designed by Perfect Design as an example, the designer designed the common strokes (Horizontal, Vertical, Left-falling, Right-falling, etc.) according to the Eight Steps of Yong, and added other strokes that would be used, such as " ⺍ ".

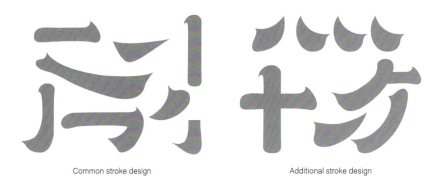

Common stroke design   Additional stroke design

Step 2. Arrange the structure

You can now arrange the fonts to be designed according to the previously designed strokes on the Mizi grid.

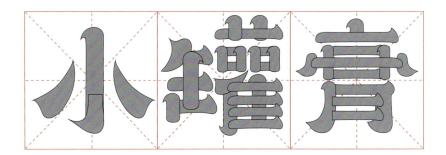

Here you can think about it: Why do we choose Mizi grid instead of the commonly used Nine-box in calligraphy? That is because the functions of two grids are different. Nine-box focuses on the stroke position while Mizi grid focuses on the structural centre. Because the primary consideration in font design is the change of font radicals and the structure core, it is recommended to use Mizi grid to arrange the strokes.

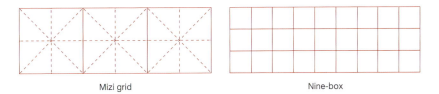

Mizi grid   Nine-box

When arranging the strokes of fonts, it is important to pay attention to the structure and core of the radicals to avoid making characters that do not look like characters. You should also learn to infer the adjustment of the proportion and thickness of the strokes in the process of placement. For example, the thickness of horizontal strokes under different structural relationships should be adjusted a little according to the actual situation, and the changed strokes should also be reflected on other similar word structures to keep font unity and connection.

For example, the distance between horizontal strokes in " 堇 " on the right side of " 罐 " was deliberately narrowed to maintain the integrity and balance between the three fonts.

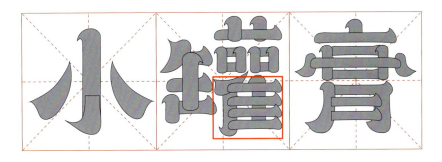

Fine-tuning of stroke details

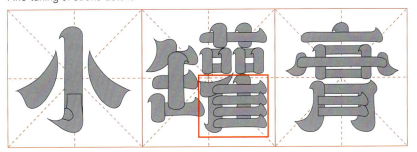

Step 3. Font Adjustment

After the overall placement and initial adjustment, the brand font has been formed at this time, but there are still detailed problems inevitably, so at this stage, it is necessary to continuously fine-tune the font, including the strokes, word space, and the core of a single word. The core of the font should be neat and unified, connect with each other, and maintain a sense of rhythm.

Remove the Mizi grid

小鑵膏

After adjusting the word space

小鑵膏

Final presentation (add the graphic logo and sub-logo)

Although the client finally chose another version of the font for commercial use, this method can still help us achieve the effect that the client wants, and at the same time it is a good design case.

After continuous practice and experimentation, Eight Steps of Yong can create many fonts with different styles but still have unity and integrity. Many font designers also use this method to design font libraries, which shows its high degree of applicability.

3.2 Stroke Design for Fonts

For the font design in the brand, the general ideas can be summarized into two types, the stroke design of the font itself and the design of the relationship between the font and the surrounding space.

3.2.1 Deformation of a single stroke

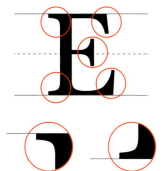

According to the previous summary of the types of fonts, except handwriting fonts, both Chinese and English fonts can be roughly divided into Serif (SimSun) and Sans-Serif (SimHei). The main difference between the two is whether the end of the stroke is marked with serif, the decorative element. Therefore, when designing fonts, you can seize this point and distort the serif at the end of the stroke to do more detailed design.

For example, The letter "E" can be designed with either Serif or Sans-Serif as its base font, and make detailed changes at the end of the stroke. But in the actual design, keep in mind the principle of integrity and maintain unity with other letters.

EME Design Studio: Eliza

Studio Caserne: Salon Panache

Björn Berglund Creative Studio: Barber Art & Crafts

(1) Reference for deformation of horizontal strokes

Overview of horizontal stroke styles

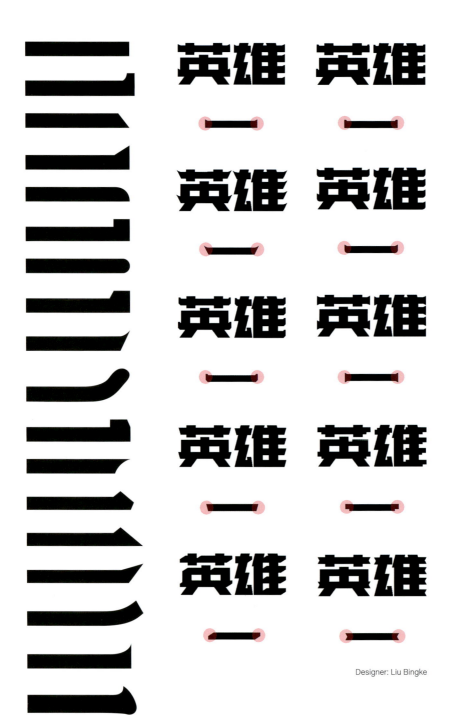

Designer: Liu Bingke

(2) Reference for deformation of vertical strokes

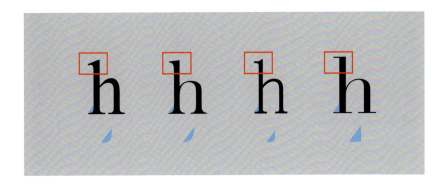

Overview of vertical stroke styles

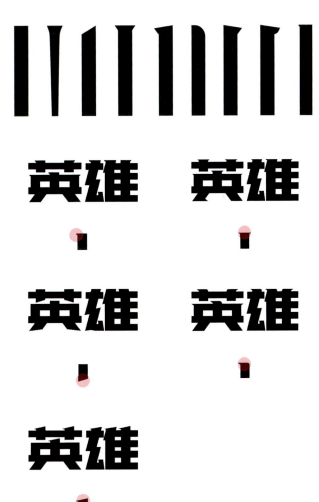

Designer: Liu Bingke

3.2.2 Angle deformation of strokes

Chinese and English fonts will pay attention to horizontal and vertical emphasis in order to ensure recognition. All strokes have certain direction rules. Therefore, the second deformation method is to change the direction angle of the strokes.

But usually, in order to ensure the overall stability, the horizontal strokes will not be changed too much. The change generally starts from the vertical stroke, left-falling stroke, right-falling stroke, or strokes with radians. For example, in the following pictures of Sakagura Cafe and V. Taste, the last stroke of the radical " 氵 " in " 酒 " and " 港 " has been bent to various degrees.

Masaomi Fujita: Sakagura Cafe

Asia One Communications Group： V·Taste

But it does not mean that horizontal strokes cannot be designed. In order to keep the characters stable, at least one direction of the horizontal and vertical strokes should be normal.

Designer: Zhao Yunsheng

Designer: Zhao Yunsheng

3.2.3 Connection and cutting of strokes

In addition to the stroke itself, the connection between the strokes (the turning point) can also have many detailed designs, such as adding a rounded turning or a chamfered design. In addition, it is also necessary to pay attention to the design of the intersection of multiple strokes. The intersection should not be too bloated, and the stroke width at the connection should be appropriately reduced.

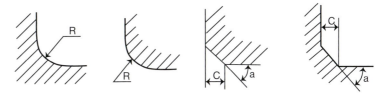

Chamfering refers to the processing step of cutting the edges and corners of the workpiece into a certain slope, and can be divided into external chamfering and internal chamfering.

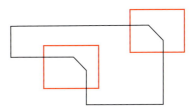

The upper right is the external chamfer, and the lower left is the internal chamfer.

Designer: Liu Bingke

Designer: Xiang Hailong

3.2.4 Ligature, broken strokes and extending strokes

(1) Ligature

Ligature refers to the fusion of strokes within or between words. Both Chinese and English fonts are suitable for connecting adjacent strokes in the same character, or connecting strokes between two characters.

Wood & Ruler Craft

Designer: Ye Wenting

Designer: Han Binghua

Designer: Liu Bingke

Xiang Hailong: L·Fish

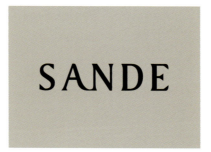

Lian Benoit: Sande Swimwear

(2) Broken strokes

Under the premise of not affecting the recognizability of the font, some strokes can be disconnected, which can also have a strong sense of form, and can also form a three-dimensional effect through broken strokes. Common broken methods include cutting along vertical or horizontal lines and using diagonal lines to separate some strokes from surrounding strokes.

Designer: Liu Bingke

In the font design of the " 翠华 ", broken strokes have been used many times, and the final blank space is combined with the background colour to produce a three-dimensional effect. When designing " 翠华 ", the designer used slashes to distinguish " 人 " on the right side in the middle of " 卒 " from other parts. However, through the method of ligature, " 人 " is connected with other parts, so as to maintain the integrity of the characters without being too scattered.

Tommy Li Design Workshop: Tsui Wah

The most important point of the broken stroke method is that it does not affect the recognizability of the font. The picture below shows the broken stroke reference of English letters. Even if part of the structure is hidden, it can still be easily distinguished because the main stroke trend is retained.

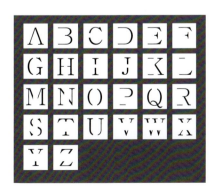

Natasha Jen: OpenView

(3) Extending stokes

Extending strokes are mainly suitable for handwriting fonts. After extending part of the strokes of the font, the overall outline of the font will change significantly and become more eye-catching. But this deformation method is too fancy and not suggested to use too much. However, the extending strokes have a unique role in maintaining the integrity and balance of the font.

For example, the handwritten "Coffee Time" designed by Marek Jagusiak. In order to form a unified rhythm with "ff", the designer deliberately extended and curved the horizontal line of "T" in the second half to maintain the unity of the font core and avoid top-heavy situations.

Designer: Marek Jagusiak

In the example below, the designer arranged the brand name "FONTEVRAUD L'ABBAYE ROYALE" in three lines, and extended the two letters "R" in the direction of the last stroke to maintain the overall balance. The designer used extending strokes to break the conventional way of design thinking, deformed the font at a vertical angle, and increased the area occupied by the font, in order to attract the attention of the audience.

When "FONTEVRAUD" is presented alone, the last stroke of the "R" is extended in both directions at the same time, maintaining the unity with the complete logo design. In addition, the vertical stroke of "R" is also intentionally omitted to avoid overly complicated visual effect.

Graphéine: Fontevraud Royal Abbey

3.3 Optical Illusion Theory: Visual Balance

To regard text as graphic design, it is necessary to look at text from the perspective of visual design, and adjust text from a more subjective visual effect.

The human eye is deceptive, and creating fonts relies more on intuition than logical thinking. If you follow precise mathematical regulations when composing, it will not look so good. Therefore, you need to be familiar with several common deceptive optical illusion theories, so that you can better understand what is wrong and what aspects can be modified in the later adjustment.

For example, the visual effect of the thickness of the same line segment is different when it is placed horizontally and when it is placed vertically. It looks thicker when placed horizontally, and thinner when placed vertically. Therefore, when designing Chinese fonts, the width of horizontal strokes can be appropriately reduced.

When two line segments of the same length are placed in a "T" cross, the line segment that is cut horizontally looks shorter.

The length of the same line segment looks different when arrows with different directions are added to the left and right ends. When the arrow is facing the line segment, the segment appears longer and visually the figure takes up more space. This is why by extending the strokes of the font, the font seems to occupy more space and achieve visual balance. Conversely, arrows pointing outward makes the line segment look shorter.

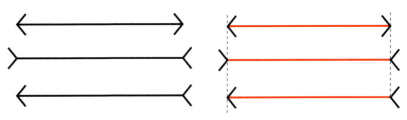

Müller-Lyer illusion

With the same height, a rectangle has a larger visual area than a circle and a triangle. Among the three shapes, only the top of the rectangle is fully filled, and the circle and triangle have visual white space around them. So, in this case, manually adjust the circle and triangle to maintain visual alignment.

For example, the size of the letters does not have to be completely designed according to the baseline and x-height. The designer needs to manually adjust the height of each letter according to the principle of "overshoot" to achieve the best visual effect.

Chapter 3
GRAPHIC DESIGN IN LOGO

1 Five Categories and Applications of Graphic Logo

1.1 Plant Logo

Applicable brands: Catering, Food

SaoPaulo is a Brazilian company that mainly sells fruit juices. Starting from the product, the designer extracted orange as the major element of the Logo, and then expressed the brand name in the hand-painted Noteworthy Light Font, showing a fresh and lively style as a whole.

Designer: Yugesh Iwaram

1.2 Animal Logo

Applicable brands: Catering, Food, Internet

From the view of marketing, animal Logos are highly recognisable, down-to-earth, and emotional, which can make the connection between brands and consumers closer. Moreover, the characteristics of some animals themselves are more in line with the products and services of the company. For example, bees represent industriousness while swans represent elegance and nobility. It is important to note that, due to cultural differences, different animals have different meanings in different countries, so it is important to bear in mind the principle of universality when designing a logo. In addition, for the future development of the company, the animal in the logo can also be considered as a mascot, satisfying the principle of adaptability in logo design.

Chetverg is an online seafood shop for fish products. The designer started with the brand's products, using fish as the main image of the Logo. In addition, fish and spoon are combined together, and four circles symbolizing bubbles and steam are added to make the Logo more vivid.

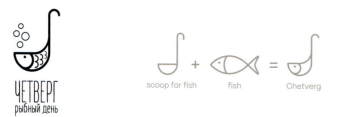

scoop for fish   fish   Chetverg

Designer: Anastasia Kurilenko

The choice of animals can not only show the products of the company, but also highlight the brand's culture.

Máxico is a travel agency whose main destination is located in a magic village in Mexico, so its brand name combines the word "Mexico" with "Mágica". As for the main graphic, the designer used the iconic animal in Colombian culture, the eagle, whose wing feathers were designed in a radial shape flying around, and the local handmade tapestry elements was also incorporated into Logo.

Design Agency: Monotypo Studio

1.3 Portrait Logo

Applicable brand: Catering

Kitano Smith Coffee is a coffee shop, as the name suggests. The graphic part of the logo is a barista operating a coffee machine, which is simple and intuitive, and emphasises the characteristics of hand-made coffee. In order to reflect the principle of adaptability of the logo, the designer has created different layouts for the graphics and text in the logo to meet the needs of different scenarios, such as the heat insulation cover of the cups and the signage at the entrance.

Design Agency: Cosydesign

1.4 Item Logo

Applicable brands: Clothing, Textiles, Daily necessities, Transportation, Architecture, Cultural

Saint Joy is a brocade satin brand founded in 1889. Rather than using cloth and brocade as the graphic elements in the Logo, it refers to several representative historical elements. The shuttle on the loom was chosen as the expression of the image, and the pattern of traditional Song brocade was added at the same time.

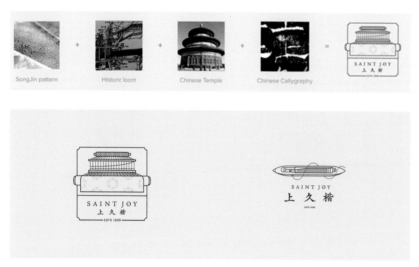

Design Agency: Juke Creative Studio

1.5 Geometric Logo

Applicable brands: Architecture, Design, Transportation

Plant, animal and portraite are all figurative graphic Logos, but there are also abstract Logos in many designs, among which the geometric Logo is the most representative one. Geometric Logos are generally composed of straight lines or curves, with certain regularity. Compared to the previous Logos, it is less emotional and is suitable for industries with a rational and stable character.

Geometric Logos often use repeated design techniques to transform a single element through rotation, symmetry, zoom-in, zoom-out, etc. to form a new image, which is a relatively easy way. The selection of elements can be the initials of the Logo or related elements.

However, it should be noted that the number of repeated elements should not be overwhelmed, and the obtained graphics should be as a whole rather than scattered patterns without a central point.

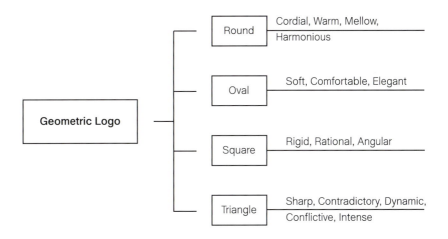

Geometric Logo	Round	Cordial, Warm, Mellow, Harmonious
	Oval	Soft, Comfortable, Elegant
	Square	Rigid, Rational, Angular
	Triangle	Sharp, Contradictory, Dynamic, Conflictive, Intense

Ocre Architecture, for example, designs the Logo as an abstract geometric square in order to create a modern and minimalistic image corresponding with the company.

Design Agency: Okta Branding

Another architectural firm, Komorebi, has adopted a similar design approach. Komorebi means "light dancing among the leaves" in Japanese, is an architecture studio that respects nature. The Logo transforms light into the geometry of the building structure, simulating the light changes in two colours from patterns to text.

Design Agency: Dmentes Estudio Creativo

2 Common Design Techniques for Graphic-Text Logo

2.1 Substitution: Substitute the Texts with Graphics

Substitution means to replace part of the elements with another one while maintaining the basic structure and characteristics of the Logo itself, thereby achieving a novel image. Since elements with different meanings are added on the original basis, more information can be conveyed through the Logo.

The designer replaced the letter "o" with simplified coffee beans, and the dot at the end reminds people with a drop of coffee at the corner of the mouth after drinking.

Design Agency: 2tigers Design Studio

Moroccan Beauty Secret is a beauty company that specialises in essential oils. From the packaging to the Logo, the water drop pattern abounds. Even the two protrusions at the top of the letter "M" are designed in the shape of water droplets. It leaves the public an initial impression that "it is related to beauty" as soon as one glances at the Logo.

MOROCCAN
BEAUTY SECRETS

Designer: Ning Li

It is also possible to replace the strokes of texts with graphics by redesigning and recombining, 壹发廊 (One Hair Salon), for instance, each stroke of the character "壹"(one) is designed in wave shape, inspired by the hair salon lamp post.

 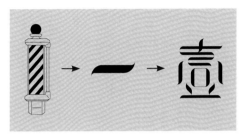

Designer: Chen Pinhan

2.2 Filling: Graphics Composed of Texts

Filling refers to filling in one or more graphics based on the outline of a graphic. By combining two or more graphics, the connection between the outer contour shape and the internal elements was made. Only the common ground of the edges of the graphics between the two elements need to be retained, and the edges of the graphics is not required to be perfectly coincident.

The Logo of Lemon Hotel is drawn by lines, showing the store names in Japanese and English at the same time. The arrangement in the shape of lemons is intuitive and vivid.

Design Agency: Takram

Eaststar Sense hopes to convey a sense of old-fashioned through the Logo. In addition to choosing the time-honored regular script as the text Logo, the designer also presents its English name "EASTSTAR" in the form of classical paper-cut for window decoration, which integrates graphics and texts.

Design Agency: Siwei Design

2.3 Positive and Negative Space: Graphics Filling Texts

Negative space is also called negative shape. In short, it is the blank part except from the major body. Take the following picture as an example. MANITÚ is the major part of the Logo, and the blank part is the negative space.

Design Agency: Dmentes Estudio Creativo

Logos based on negative space design can express meaning in the major part while display the content in the blank space. The combination of the two parts can create a Logo with a simple shape but rich implied meanings.

Through the transformation between positive and negative space, the visual symbols can be strengthened, the viewer's association can be aroused, the interest can be enhanced, and the viewer's memory of the Logo can be refreshed. It is also a good way to combine graphics with texts. Excellent positive and negative space Logo design should consider the correlation between elements and the degree of fitness of public lines. Forcing the correlation for uniqueness may result in opposite effect. In addition, the same element can be expressed in different ways, such as circular, triangular, square... The suitable shapes need to be selected in terms of the blank space in the main part.

In the case of Petion, the designer has fitted the silhouette of a pet dog to the counter of the letter P. However, this method does not suitable for letter "e" and "o".

Designer: Vinay Gowtham M

Substitution, filling, positive and negative space are all design methods under the concept of isomorphism. A simple understanding of isomorphism is combining different elements into a new one.We should emphasise the correlation between elements, and avoid stacking elements and redundant design when designing.

Designer: Péter Vasvári

3 Logo in Grid/Diagram

There are many different styles of grid paper commonly used by designers. These grids are used to regulate the size, position, distance, length, proportions and angles of the logo, reminding us of taking notice of the details.

Designers will use circles, ellipses, arcs, lines, triangles and other geometric figures to assist in the design of the logo, and adjust the design subtly to make sure every bevel, radian, spacing and proportion unified and beautiful. In this way, the Logo seems more comfortable.

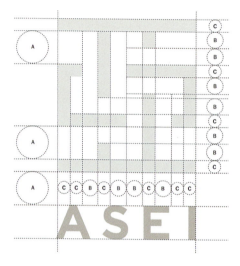

Design Agency: Tegusu

Designer: Simon Laliberté

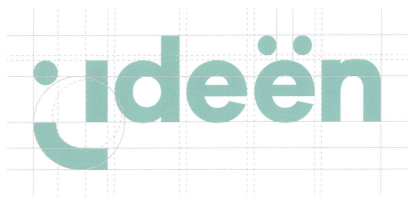

Design Agency: The Branding People

Design Agency: Juke Creative Studio

Analysing the drawing with ruler and compass by other designers helps us to think about the forming process of a Logo, starting from large surface and decomposing the details step by step. By applying Boolean operations, the complex graphics can be divided into simple ones, instead of adjusting the anchor points with the pen tool painfully.

Design Agency: Form & Function

In addition, Logo in grid/diagram can presents the process of drawing. The auxiliary lines in the graphics can, to a certain extent, help the designer to explain the design concept and the design approach, which will make the work more convincing and more acceptable to the client. However, Logo in grid/diagram is not suitable for every type of Logo, such as realistic one, calligraphy one or handwriting one.

Design Agency: Heavy Mx

Design Agency: Slwei Design

Design Agency: Never-Never

3.1 The Golden Ratio

The golden ratio,1:0.618, is a reference ratio preferred by designers and is known as "the ratio number of the most aesthetically meaning". It is widely applied in art, colour, design, architecture even music. However, the golden ratio does not ensure the perfect proportion of the Logo, nor apply to every edge of all Logos. It is just a reference. therefore, designers still need to use visual judgement to determine size, position and proportion in many cases.

3.1.1 How to draw a golden ratio circle

1. Draw a square.

2. Duplicate the square and modify the length of the top and bottom sides to 1.618 times the original side length.

3. Adjust the position of the two rectangles to make the left side overlapped.

4. Draw a square inside a rectangle, and so on in a similar fashion.

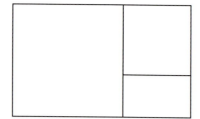

As long as the canvas is large enough, it can be drawn indefinitely, resulting in squares and rectangles of various sizes, all rectangles with a length-to-width ratio of 1.618:1.

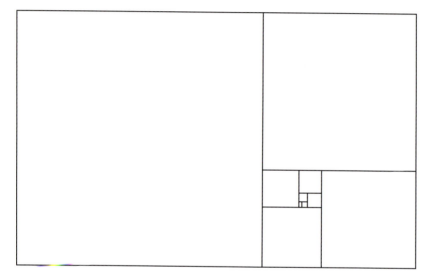

5. Select the ellipse tool, then hold down "Alt+Shift" at the center of the square, meanwhile, drag the mouse so as to draw a circle to fit the side of the square.

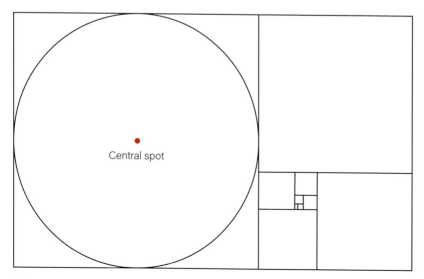

Central spot

6. Draw circles of different sizes in the square frame in turn and stack them together.

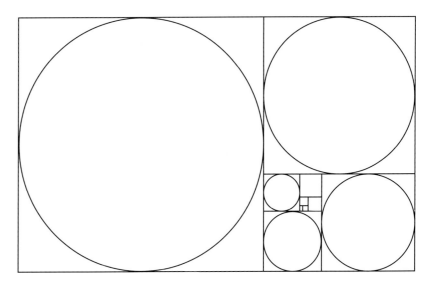

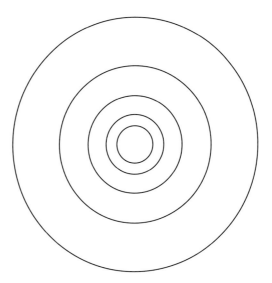

7. Finally, select a suitable circle, and fit the arc to the edge of the sketch one by one, and then adjust it according to the actual situation.

3.2 Boolean Operations

Boolean operations are derived from the logical deduction method of numerical symbolisation, including union, intersection, and subtraction. To put it in an easier way to understand, it is the addition and subtraction between graphics. There are 10 operations in the Pathfinder in Adobe Illustrator.

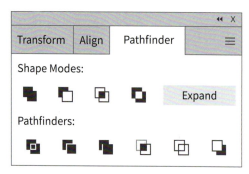

Ctrl+Shift+F9

Shape Modes:

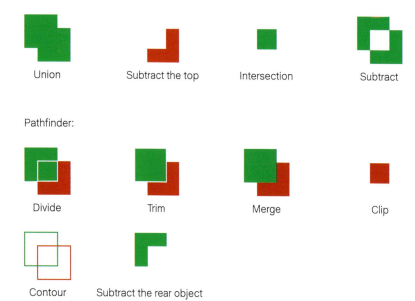

Union   Subtract the top   Intersection   Subtract

Pathfinder:

Divide   Trim   Merge   Clip

Contour   Subtract the rear object

Chapter 4
COLOURS OF LOGO

1 Hue Scheme

1.1 Hue

Hue refers to the outer phase of a colour, the different colours reflected or projected onto an object as perceived by the human eye when illuminated by different wavelengths of light. In simple terms, hue is the name given to the various colours. Hue is the primary characteristic of colour and the most intuitive criterion for distinguishing between colours. Hue is measured by position in the hue ring from 0 degrees to 360 degrees.

Hue circle

1.2 Hue Colour Scheme

1.2.1 Monochromatic

A monochromatic colour scheme is one in which a single hue is used, with variations in saturation and brightness. For example, the Matchaki Matcha logo is mainly green, with different saturations and brightnesses chosen to keep the whole unified and create a fresh and natural look.

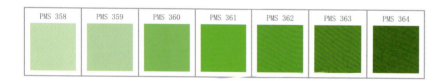

PMS 331	PMS 332	PMS 333	PMS Green	PMS 334	PMS 335	PMS 336
PMS 337	PMS 338	PMS 339	PMS 340	PMS 341	PMS 342	PMS 343
PMS 3375	PMS 3385	PMS 3395	PMS 3405	PMS 3415	PMS 3425	PMS 3435
PMS 344	PMS 345	PMS 346	PMS 347	PMS 348	PMS 349	PMS 350
PMS 351	PMS 352	PMS 353	PMS 354	PMS 355	PMS 356	PMS 357
PMS 358	PMS 359	PMS 360	PMS 361	PMS 362	PMS 363	PMS 364
PMS 365	PMS 366	PMS 367	PMS 368	PMS 369	PMS 370	PMS 371
PMS 372	PMS 373	PMS 374	PMS 375	PMS 376	PMS 377	PMS 378
PMS 379	PMS 380	PMS 381	PMS 382	PMS 383	PMS 384	PMS 385

| PMS 358 | PMS 359 | PMS 360 | PMS 361 | PMS 362 | PMS 363 | PMS 364 |

MATCHAKI

Primary Matcha Color
C89 M44 Y76 K45
R7 G75 B58
#074b3a

Primary Matcha Color
C66 M0 Y85 K0
R80 G197 B93
#50c55d

Primary Matcha Color
C2 M2 Y2 K0
R249 G245 B244
#f9f5f4

Design Agency: Monajans

1.2.2 Analogous

On hue rings spaced 30 degrees apart, analogous colour schemes are usually defined as colours spaced 60 to 90 degrees apart. The combination of similarly coloured objects often makes for a more harmonious image. The logo of Soo Zee 23 , for example, is based on the brand colours of red, yellow and orange. By choosing two different colours, the "Z" and "E" in "Soo Zee" are combined with " 二三 " . The integrity of the letters is maintained while reflecting the additional meaning.

Design Agency: The Creative Method

(Eat)

(Twenty Three)

1.2.3 Square

Square scheme is colour combination that are 90 degrees on the hue ring. In this colour scheme, the colour differences are clearer and the colour contrasts are more prominent, resulting in a stronger visual tension.

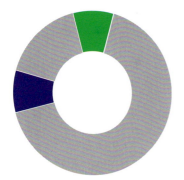

Blue-green matching

Red-yellow matching

Orange-purple matching

An example of this is IVAJ from Valencia, a public service provider for young people. In their branding scheme, the designers have used purple, orange and green as the main colours, which is one of the more common square scheme.

1.2.4 Complementary

In the hue ring, colours separated by 180°are called complementary colour, and the common complementary colour schemes are blue-orange, red-green and yellow-violet.

Blue-orange complementation

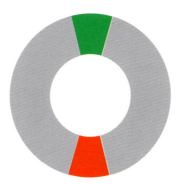

Red-green complementation

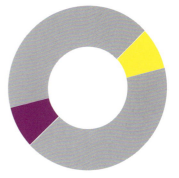

Yellow-purple complementation

The use of complementary colours in a logo design can create a special visual contrast and balance, adding vibrancy to the work and making the logo appear more lively. An example of this is the project Khoil, a spontaneous renovation of a disused factory, led by young people who have returned to their hometown. The designer has adopted blue as the standard colour and infused it with yellow to represent the power of youth. The contrasting colours symbolise the vibrant newness of the old industrial space.

Design Agency: 3&4 Design Studio

The proportions of complementary colours are also important; if two colours are in equal or similar proportions, the contrast will appear too strong. In the picture below, the red and green colours are too evenly proportioned and dazzling.

As a rule of thumb, most designers prefer a ratio of 3:7 or 2:8 for colour distribution.

2 Tone scheme

2.1 Tone

Tone refers to the relative intensity, strength and shade of an image. It is not a certain property of a colour, but rather the basic tendency of a colour's appearance and a generalisation of the colour. Hue is usually expressed as a combination of saturation and brightness, and adjusting both results in a richer variation of colour.

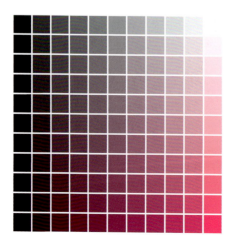

2.2 Tonal colour scheme

2.2.1 Saturation comparison

The saturation of a colour refers to the vibrancy or intensity of the colour, which is the proportion of the primary colour in the colour. The proportion of neutral grey in a hue will affect its saturation. As saturation decreases, the colour will become lighter. The colour system is often expressed in terms of saturation, while the saturation of black and white can be referred to as greyscale.

The higher the saturation of the colour, the more vibrant it is, and vice versa, the lighter it is.

For example, in the logo design for the chocolate brand Xocola, the designer chose black as the main colour, with a clean and simple colour style and a clean serif font to achieve an aesthetic and balance, with the finishing touch being the bright yellow in the secondary colour. The bright yellow is the accent colour in the overall visual, contrasting with the other colours on the packaging. This difference in saturation creates a strong visual impact on the logo and helps to create a striking impression.

Primary

C75 M68 Y67 K90
R0 G0 B0
#000000

Secondary

C0 M6 Y88 K0
R255 G240 B31
#FFFF01F

C0 M0 Y0 K0
R255 G255 B255
#FFFFFF

Designer: Kimmy Lee

2.2.2 Brightness comparison

The brightness of a colour can also be understood as the luminosity of the colour. The variability in brightness can be seen in the same hue or in different hues. By adding different proportions of black or white to a colour, the brightness will change. The more black is added, the lower the brightness, while the opposite is true for white.

The brighter the colour, the closer it is to white, while the lower the brightness, the closer it is to black.

The primary and secondary colours used in the design of the Asei Architects logo, for example, are black and white with varying shades of mint blue, evoking the colours of natural things such as water and air. This colour palette echoes the firm's philosophy of empowering architecture and giving people a renewed sense of their environment. This colour scheme will naturally draw attention to the brighter logo when looking at the brand's materials.

Primary

C13 M0 Y6 K100   C0 M0 Y0 K0

Secondary

C13 M0 Y6 K40   C13 M0 Y6 K0

Design Agency: Tegusu

Chapter 5
CASE STUDIES

1 Design Ideas in Details

Logo design in branding should not just be about learning techniques and indiscriminately using your favourite variations in your work. If you only focus on showing off the techniques in your daily design practice, but do not really combine your thoughts on the brand with the logo design, you will end up with a flashy piece of work that does not add commercial value to the brand and will not impress the brand owner, let alone the consumer.

Advanced designers usually think more about how to integrate the logo with the brand's emotions, and focus more on the emotions conveyed by the logo rather than the formality of the design itself. Regardless of the technique used, the ultimate goal is to communicate the values of the brand through the logo and to create a design that is eye-catching.

In order to give you a deeper understanding of the design of a logo in a brand, this book takes emotion as the entry point and presents the following three case studies, analysing in detail the process of designing each piece from scratch and its design characteristics, as a reference for similar styles of design.

1.1 Localization of Foreign Cultures: London Tonkotsu Ramen Chain Store

Design Agency: Something More Near
Creative Director: David Gunn
(Something More Near)
Designer: Tomomi Maezawa, Adam Johnson
Client: Tonkotsu

Step 1. Investigate

Tonkotsu is the leading ramen brand in the London restaurant market. As its business grew, Tonkotsu wanted to update its brand image, emphasizing the complex cultural characteristics of the combination of modern Japan and modern London.

From the noodle machine to the ramen bowls in the restaurant, everything conveys Tonkotsu's passion for the craft of ramen, hoping to provide customers with a unique, modern ramen experience.

Passion for Japanese ramen

Modern restaurant in London

In Japanese, the restaurant's name Tonkotsu refers to a type of ramen made with tonkotsu (which means pork-bone in Japanese) soup. The key challenge of this brand refresh was therefore to break through the stereotypes of the pork-bone ramen style and create a unique and modern brand imageThe key challenge of this brand refresh was therefore to break through the stereotypes of the pork-bone ramen style and create a unique and modern brand imageThe key challenge of this brand update was therefore to break through the stereotypes of the pork-bone ramen style and create a unique and modern brand image. This change has been recognized by all parties including consumers who are familiar with ramen culture.

Step 2. Design

How to use a visual language compatible with modern Japan and modern London to express the brand's dedication to ramen culture? The designers explored from the perspective of graphic design.

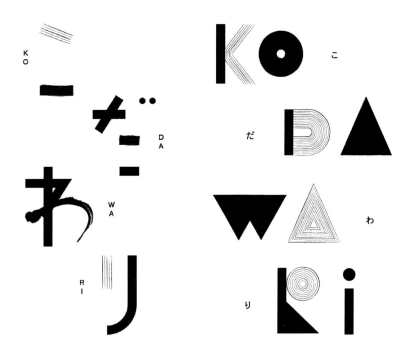

Geometric figures representing Western elements   Calligraphic textures representing Japanese elements

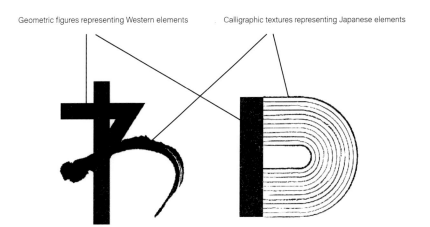

Geometric figures represent Western aesthetics, while the handcrafted texture in the design represents the Japanese calligraphic art. The combination of the two elements creates a modern style of cultural fusion.

In Japanese, Tonkotsu is a combination of two words. Ton for pork and Kotsu for bone. However, the single word Kotsu also signifies the inner spirit and core idea of things. As a result, the designers used the Japanese glyph of "Kotsu" to design a recognizable logo. For the audience who knows Japanese, this logo can also give them a clear understanding of the restaurant's brand tone.

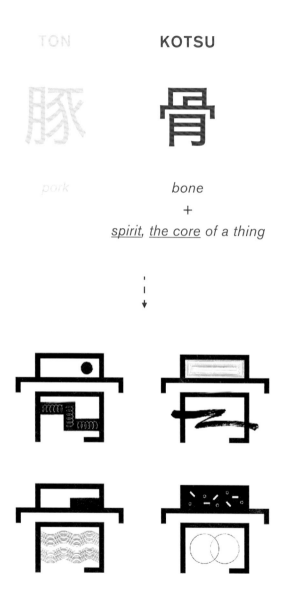

TON

KOTSU

pork

bone

+

<u>*spirit*</u>, <u>*the core*</u> *of a thing*

Step 3. Apply

Consumers are very fond of logo designs centred on the "Kotsu" glyph. Therefore, the designers decided to follow the trend and incorporate the brand name "Tonkotsu" into it as a brand trademark.

They also designed cross-cultural noodle elements and tableware elements for different decorative scenes.

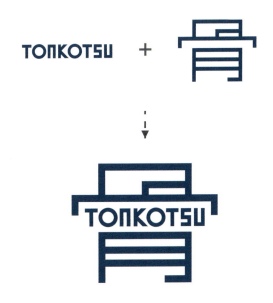

In addition, the trendy fluorescent colour, combined with the use of indigo blue, which is commonly used in ramen shops, creates a new colour combination.

The designers combined fluorescent colours with more concise wordmarks based on customers' suggestions for design details. The well-designed logo is a tribute to customers who understand Japanese culture. At the same time, the bold, unique icon design is especially noticeable in digital promotional backgrounds and various print materials.

1.2 American Rock Tea: Rock Juice

When rock meets tea, it is a brand new attempt for both image promotion and brand management. How to combine tea, American street culture and rock themes, and at the same time be suitable for Chinese market, is the core work of this project.

Designer: Liuxun

First, analyse visual features and refine keywords:
Tea + Rock + American street + Monster + Cool

The core material of tea foods: tea and liquid.

Representative elements of rock culture: Metal rivets and electric guitars.

Monster image related to tea: Pi Xiu, the auspicious beast of tea.

The designers have obtained a number of scattered information and thoughts, which need to be selected and integrated in the next step.

The catering industry is typically dominated by offline experience. The most effective visual medium for consumers to obtain brand information in a dazzling market is text. Therefore, textual vision is particularly important for catering brands. This case will also consider text as the core visual driver, and the graphic as a visual symbol for auxiliary performance.

Through research and analysis, rock and American street culture have similarities, which are aggressive, freedom, wild, etc. Therefore, the designers reset the text to increase the core and make it taller based on the full and thick Sans Serif, adding a rebellious temperament. At the same time, the designers added more strokes to letters and characters with fewer strokes. On the contrary, they reasonably omitted strokes of letters and characters with more strokes to achieve visual balance.

ROCK JUICE 茶震兽
ROCK JUICE 茶震兽

After the balanced and tough text structure is built, it is necessary to further adjust the shape. Referring to the representative elements of rock culture, metal rivets, sharp corners are added to the text design to strengthen the rock punk temperament.

Tea is a combination of fresh beverages and tea. Its ingredients have the characteristics of natural elements and hand-brewing. Rock and American streets have a sense of age, and they both have attributes of historical and cultural precipitation. The designers further depicted the details and created a retro mottled text temperament, corresponding to the handmade freshness and cultural background.

ROCK JUICE 茶震兽
ROCK JUICE 茶震兽

Monsters were originally intended to be dreadful and strange creatures. In the modern age where various cultures such as literature, history, music, films and videos are blended, monsters have gradually become a fashionable element that shows individuality. American street culture is a diverse mixture related to tattoos, Old School, motorcycles, rock, etc. The designers investigated some patterns of these monsters and beasts for reference.

Monochromatic, power and darkness are the comprehensive characteristics of this type of graphics. Therefore, they used the Pi Xiu as the base image to draw several series of monster graphics for Rock Juice.

The forehead of the Pi Xiu is composed of leaves, and the outer side is added with a circular moiré pattern with traditional cultural attributes. But this is not obvious enough, it is quite different from the shape of conventional tea, and the temperament is too dull and depressing.

In the second edition, the Pi Xiu's beard and hair are drawn into the image of leaves, which are closer to the shape of tea leaves and more prominent. The mouth of Pi Xiu is open and roaring, which makes it no longer dull and depressing. But the overall temperament is slightly fierce, and there is still a difference between cool and terrifying.

The third edition retains the setting of the hair of PI Xiu drawn as leaves in the second edition, plus the setting of the spring water flowing out of the closed mouth, while simplifying the head modeling, so that readers focus on the theme of "tea + water = PI Xiu". It seems to meet the needs of visual symbols, but at the same time, it shows vicissitudes. Too much beard and hair makes it look like an old man, or we should say, an old Pi Xiu. It is significantly different from the positioning of popular and cool effect.

With the above unsatisfactory manuscripts, it is found that the problem lies in two points:
1. The overall temperament needs to be younger and simplified;
2. The elements of tea are too prominent, which will weaken the recognition of Pi Xiu or lead to far-fetched and insufficient in aesthetics.

The designers used divergent thinking once again and drawing on the shape characteristics of the lion dance in Guangdong: powerful, energetic and friendly. The re-drawing combined the face shape of the lion with the Pi Xiu, and cleverly used the tea leaves as the ears. The image of Pi Xiu with a simpler shape looks young, full of vitality, and also has affinity, which is closer to the ideal.

It needs to be further adjusted and refined to achieve a more simple and meticulous effect, while continuing the retro mottled effect of the text.

The identification information, youth, coolness, Pi Xiu, and tea, is satisfied, but there is still a lack of colour changes. The sharp corners of the Pi Xiu are embellished with green as the core visual point to strengthen the identification features. At the same time, it corresponds to the rivets style in the text design.

In the era of the Republic of China, where productivity and execution were insufficient, the production effect of rich colours could not be achieved. Most of the prints are designed in one colour or two colours, forcing the picture design to be simple and pure. The changes of black, white and gray are also mainly in monochrome design, but at the same time, it also achieves unique visual beauty and style attributes. These are in line with the visual positioning of Rock Juice.

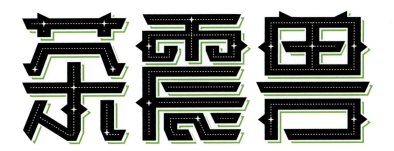

Catering brands are one of the industries where consumers interact with the brand products in the space for the longest time. A flexible and practical application system will enhance the brand's memory and recognition. The brand name is richly designed in a two-tone colour mode, giving it a punk street feel with a retro vibe. This text-centred design combines brand text content with elements of street culture, tea and rock & roll, making it a very meaningful reference case.

1.3 Japanese Modern Minimalism: Miamanday

Design Agency: 3&4 Design Studio
Designer: Chen Pinhan
Client: Miamanday

Miamanday sets 4 consumption scenarios: commuters ordering; take-out orders for meeting meals; family dinner takeaway; dinner options preferred by family elders.

For the logo design, the client sought a Japanese and modern minimalist style. The designer combined the character "鰻" with the image of an eel, striving for the coexistence of lightness and stability.

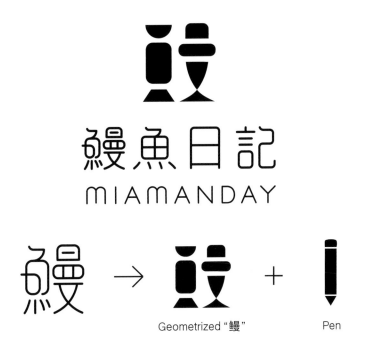

Geometrized "鰻"   Pen

The designers take the main image of "鰻" as the brand identity, combining the slippery posture of the eel's body as a font design expression, introducing the concept of pictographs, turning the designed text outline into geometric surfaces, and combining with the representative object "pen" of writing diaries.

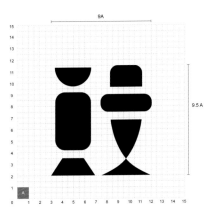

In order to meet different usage scenarios, the graphic logo, and Chinese and English names of Miamanday have been made into two different versions, horizontally and vertically.

The choice of main colour system and auxiliary colour system:

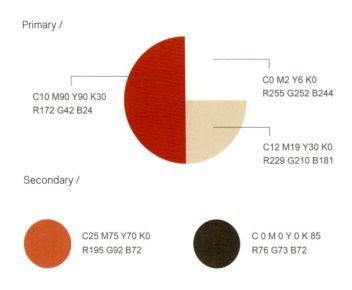

Primary /

C10 M90 Y90 K30
R172 G42 B24

C0 M2 Y6 K0
R255 G252 B244

C12 M19 Y30 K0
R229 G210 B181

Secondary /

C25 M75 Y70 K0
R195 G92 B72

C 0 M 0 Y 0 K 85
R76 G73 B72

The auxiliary graphics of the Miamanday are also changed according to the graphic logo to maintain the visual unity of the brand.

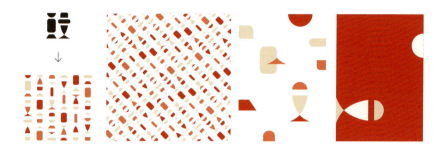

The designers also designed extended use colours for the brand. From Monday to Sunday, there are different colour systems every day, so that customers can always keep fresh.

Staff Horizontal Business Card /

2 Case Studies

Represent

(A) Name	(C) Description	(E) Font & Typeface	(G) Logo in Grid
(B) Information	(D) Colour Scheme	(F) Logo	(H) Application

Note: Colour Scheme marked with an asterisk (*) in D have been compiled by the editors for reference only.

Nigma — High End Street Wear Genderless Brand

Design Agency: Okta Branding & Design
Project Manager & Copywriter: Camila Chisini
Art Director: Camila Chisini
Designer: Camila Chisini e Lara Rei
Photography: Nomma Media
Client: Nigma (Sthéfani Pietrowski)

Nigma is a high end street wear genderless brand that exists to break stereotypes. It's a way of expression that's completely free from prejudice. Our challenge was to understand the bold and provocative essence of the brand to express in an aggressive and strong visual identity. We've built a visual universe with a rebellious and aggressive personality. We've created a short and strong name, developed an unconventional logo and drawn textures that refer to the "street style", becoming a unique form of expression.

Fonts: Minim; Roboto Slab; Montserrat
Typeface Styles: Sans-Serif; Slab Serif

BRAND NAME PROCESS

250 NAMES

ODD
ROOT INDE RAPA IGNOT MATIZ YOLO VERT FOLK WTF
BASE VENIDA BUQUÊ TRETA VIANA FITA STRAT LOOSE AFIM
STRT TRAJO NONAME SARARÁ RUPTURA PRISMAS RETRATO FLECHA VIBEAT OMNE GNOTSUP
ALMA CRUISIN AVENIDA SUBSOMA MUTANTE SEMSENSO ROLÉ LATITUDE VERTER ANEXO SENSO NAIPE
FACE CULTURB SUBVEST RESPONSA SELF-RULE CONTRAJE TRUSENSE MAGMA SALVE ETNA
INDEF CORAGEM NAMELESS TRICKSTER LADO STREEDOM NIGMA CALÇADA POLISENSO VERSAVICE DAORA
CAPUTMATIZANTE MESCLADO VICEVERSA URBITTUDE ALTERSENSO DEGRADÊ FRONTJUMP TAGGIN
GYÖK MUNIÇÃO PETULANCIA SINCRÉTICO TROPICALIA INSOLENCIA CONTRA-TRAJE AS-MINA-OS-MANO FAUNOS
CARTOLA INDEPENDENTE CADA-UM-COM-SEU-CORRE ROUTE FLOW ANAGRAMA CENA-UNDERGROUND
INDEXO PANOMANO SUBURBANO MATIZADO KNOWLEDGE-WAVE TRIZ AMBISENSO
STRA DUPLO SUBVERSO SEM-SURA PRISMANTE VIRSAVECE MISCELÂNEA NEMSENSO OBSCEMOS SUBVESTIR ESCUDO
EIXO SELVA MESCLA CÔNCAVO OBSCERNO VIRSAVECE NONSENSE ORDINARIO URBANUS GLÓRIA CAFUSO
VIÉS ALTER RIZOMA PRISMA UR SUBURBA CARAI OBLÍQUO THA-HOOD FLANELA URBCULT SQUAD SARAU
RIMA ONDA GUME AMBITO OBSCENO DESVIÉS ARRANJOCIVES AVESSO CURVA MONO
WIDE PREZA NOSIDE STRATO INEXATO ALLEY UEOU RUNA INDEP

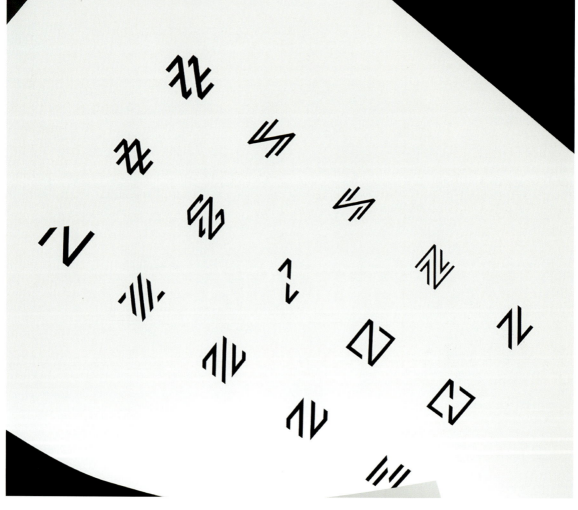

The Crux & Co.

Design Agency: Hue Studio
Project Manager & Copywriter: Vian Risanto
Art Director: Vian Risanto
Designer: Vian Risanto
Photography: Jave Hooni
Client: Kevin Li

The Crux & Co. is a 270 sqm Café and patisserie situated on the ground floor of The Emerald Apartments in South Melbourne. The Crux & Co. is 60% casual 40% classy and 50% chit 50% chat. They say life is all about balance and that is the crux of the branding.

From the monogram logo which resemblance the percentage symbol and a series of C/C tag lines are all balanced out by the pattern streamlined across all artwork and packaging. Custom designed typeface was developed for a family of logo type which featured on each packaging.

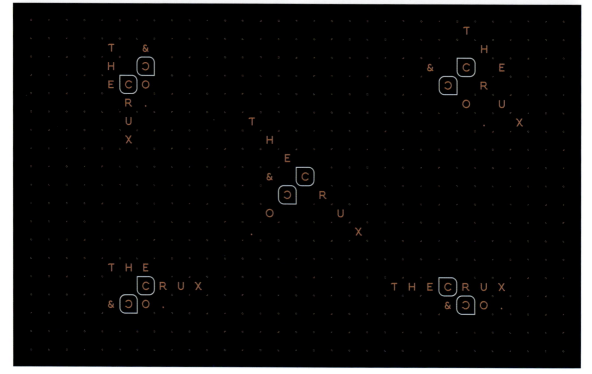

Fonts: Custom made font; Edmond Sans (Regular, Medium, Bold)
Typeface Style: Sans-Serif

Garna Xang Cocina Asia / Mx.

Design Agency: Henriquez Lara Estudio

Project Manager & Copywriter:
Javier Henríquez Lara, Iván Soto Camba

Art Director: Javier Henríquez Lara

Designer: Marycarmen Terán, Lorena Lozano,
Mariana Núñez, José Pablo Salazar, Javier Henriquez Lara

Ceramic Design: Javier Henriquez Lara

Photography: David Jilkyns

Illustrator: Javier Henríquez Lara, Marycarmen Teran Sanz

Client: Garna Xang

The space at Garna Xang seems to fold like a tortilla, so Mexican and Asian cultures could meet. This is not a fusion but confusion between Asia and Mexico.

The typeface of the logo was created exclusively for the Brand, inspired in symbols of oriental writing. We were also looking for a font that could find an original balance with Mexican illustrations and references. With that combination we create a fun and polite character for the brand.

Auxiliary font DIN creates a current and fresh look. Trough shapes and composition brand personality is enforced.

Font: DIN Bold Alt
Typeface Style: Sans-Serif

ERROR 404: SUERTE NO ENCONTRADA

TU FORTUNA ESTÁ EN OTRA GALLETA

ENCONTRARÁS CALCETÍN PERDIDO

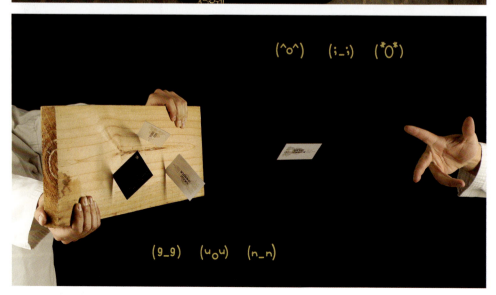

Gala Sushi

Project Manager & Copywriter: Dmitry Neal
Art Director: Dmitry Neal
Designer: Dmitry Neal
Client: Gala

Gala is a sushi bar in Tallinn. The main emphasis in new corporate style was made on shape and colour. We went back from solutions typical of Japanese cuisine. Instead simple geometric shapes and bright open colours were used as the basis. Their combination and collaboration allowed us to achieve a contrasting and memorable visual effect.

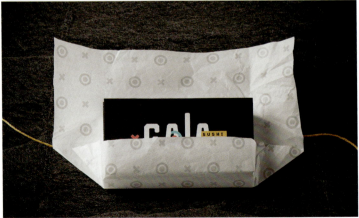

Fonts: Intro; Gotham pro
Typeface Styles: Sans-Serifs; Blackletter

Zanzan Eyewear Rebrand

Design Agency: STUDIO L'AMI
Designer: Fredericus L'AMI
Photography: Fredericus L'AMI
Client: Zanzan

Inspired by classic Italian coastal motifs, the rebrand of Zanzan relaunches this iconic eyewear brand as they extend their product range to include optical & mens collections in 2018.

The dynamic Zanzan striped logotype is at the heart of the identity system. Elements of the original mark needed to be retained for continuity and the new logotype had to appeal to a wider audience of men & women. We introduced a series of graphic marks inspired by iconic parasol silhouettes that delineate Zanzan optical & sun collections through a simple graphic system that operates above (sun) and below (optical) the logotype.

Hand-made in Italy

Fonts: Futura PT; Aldine 721; Cutive Mono
Typeface Styles: Sans-serif (Futura PT); Serif (Aldine 721); Monotype (Cutive Mono)

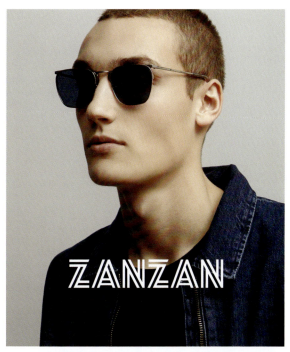

A vibrant core colour family with seasonal shifts operates alongside pattern and a versatile approach to typography — this ensures playful elements are easily retained throughout the identity application. While we didn't design Zanzan's online store, identity elements, approach to typography and colour palette ensure it's consistent with the overall Zanzan experience.

Barber Art & Crafts

Design Agency: Björn Berglund Creative Studio
Project Manager & Copywriter: Caroline Gustafsson, Björn Berglund
Art Director: Björn Berglund
Designer: Björn Berglund
Photography: Sofia Johnsson
Client: Barber Art & Crafts

Designer wanted to find a balance between tradition and modern thinking, and combining the male audience in the age of 30 to 45 years old with the warmth of the female founder of Barber. A strict male look combined with a female curved way. The solution is a symmetric composition with capital letters with serifs that signals confidence and pride. To soften the overall composition, designer has added a curvaceous line at centre line. The designer wanted the logo to be fresh when used in a variety of contexts. Stylish, vintage and clean, but also warm and inviting. The logo is easy to recognize and remember, even in cost-effective one colour print.

Fonts: Utopia for copy; Handmade typography (lettering) for Barber letters
Typeface Style: Serif

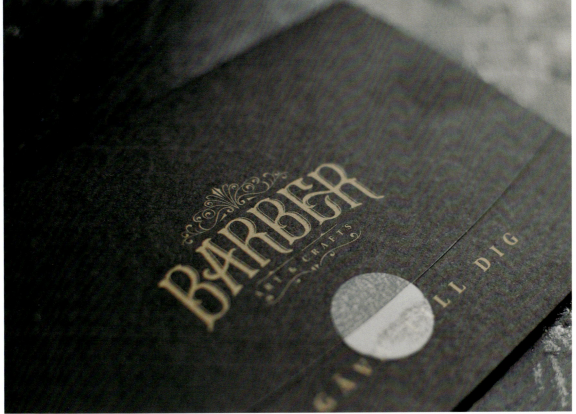

ENJOY A CLEAN CUT.

*Typeface
for headlines:*
Utopia Bold

*Typeface
for bodytext:*
Utopia Regular

Ed molligenda vent qui dolorit aut as dero invene cores illignim arum adionseque sinissum remo endae volupta tectur, sum volut qui ut fuga. Re mollece rferia volupis archillam nonse dollam nus sint officto tatectium audi accuptam etur aut utem id eictati aut modis se dempore mporitatet inus earum ex et preptatior si ut endios aut et am, ut eos aut imaioriores mo endi aboribus eosam, volorendit alignimin rem adis solenis doluptis amusdande nus doluptatibus doluptat.

Key words
for the typography
of Barber Art & Crafts:

Boldness
(headlines in capital
letters for a powerful
expression)

Centered composition
(signals confidence and
stability)

Simplicity
(one font in two
different weights gives a
calmness to the type)

THE BOX OF TOOLS

Symbol   *The paper (Munken Pure)*   *The Arc*   *Warm greyscale imagery*

The logo   *Decorative elements*   *The colors.*   *Texture*

Orland

Design Agency: Bullseye
Client: Orland

Orland, with nautical inspirations, represents a shoe range applied to this theme. Crafted from noble materials, Orland is a premium footwear for the daily lifestyle.

The bonding with this nautical style was applied to Orland's identity, with warm beach tones, and proper graphic elements from the seamanship communication.

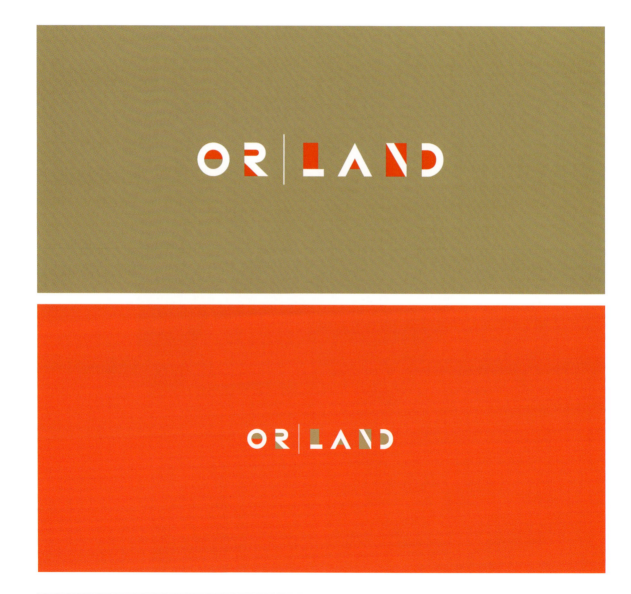

Fonts: Bifur; Bebas Neue
Typeface Style: Sans-Serif

The construction of the logo was an created typography combining the brands name with their market lifestyle. A rebranding project with a purpose in giving a new identity related to sailing and ocean themes. For that reason, and based in the nautical lighthouses of the sea front, the logo's typography was built in layers.

Meissl & Schadn — Schnitzel Love

Design Agency: Moodley Brand Identity

Project Manager & Copywriter: Laura Kalcher, Severin Corti, Sabrina Luttenberger

Art Director: Natascha Triebl

Designer: Natascha Triebl, Lena Wurm, Susanne Prinik, Alex Muralter

Photography: Michael Königshofer

Client: Weitzer Hotels BetriebsgesmbH

The legendary name Meissl & Schadn that stands for everything that once made the Viennese cuisine famous. The new Meissl & Schadn is where old meets new and classiness meets smartness. This is why the Corporate Design combines classic elements with unconventional ones. Fresh pink greets dapper gold and fonts are used extensively. No surprise, since the font "Romana" is used again in the new design — after it was originally used in the Meissl & Schadn's menu at the turn of the century. The restaurant's tradition becomes as visible as the Austrian's love to Schnitzel. There is a classic typography that gets its bold presence in the Corporate Design. The Gill Sans, in some sort of three dimensional Ultra Bold, makes for a glamorous appearance of the "Schnitzel love".

Fonts: Romana; Gill sans

Typeface Styles: Sans-Serif; Script

Die Einladung

Meissl & Schadn

Grand Opening

SIE SIND HERZLICH EINGELADEN

SCHNITZEL LOVE

Meissl & Schadn

Meissl & Schadn
WIEN

TRUE SCHNITZEL MAKER

ZERTIFIKAT / CERTIFICATE

...r liebste Musik.

MHHH ...
#HAD
SCHNITZEL
TODAY

, 1010 Vienna

schadn.at

Salon Panache

Design Agency: Studio Caserne
Art Director: Vedran Vaskovic, Léo Allaire, Ugo Varin
Designer: Vedran Vaskovic
Client: Salon Panache

The celebrated Panache salon wished to redo its visual identity to better represent the innovative spirit that colours all its haircuts and the reputation that it has built since it opened its doors in 2011. Inspired by the motion of scissors, the new identity proudly features a diagonal line created through typographic work. The diagonal acts as a subtle visual signature throughout the salon, accessorizing the space's design.

Font: Brutal Type
Typeface Styles: Serif; Sans-Serif

Qleaners

Design Agency: Anagrama Studio
Creative Direction: Mike Herrera
Photography: Caroga Foto
Client: Qleaners

The corporate identity's guiding concept is inspired by classic fashion brands. The custom logo serif typeface can't be missed, as it simulates organic shapes like the ones created by moving water. Adding to the organic brand behavior, strokes with thick beginnings and thin endings are employed. The secondary typography is characterized by a condensed style contributing to a modern balance in contrast with the classic logotype tone. The dynamic typographic dispositions respond to the sizes of spaces and materials in the brand collateral.

The colour palette varies in the ranges of green and blue behaving consistently with the "cleanliness" and "freshness" brand values. These green and blue tones co-exist with white spaces and black elements that are characteristic in the high-end fashion industry.

Font: Modified Pistilli Roman
Typeface Style: Sans-Serif

Qleaners

PERFECCIÓN EN LAVADO EN SECO

NUEVA COSTERA NO.4050   NO. 4050
SANTIAGO DE CHILE
TEL. 600 766 0000 / 600 778 0000

Qleane

QLEANERS.COM
VICTOR@QLEANERS.COM

Qleaners

PERFECCIÓN EN LAVADO EN SECO

NUEVA COSTERA NO.4050   NO. 4050
SANTIAGO DE CHILE
TEL. 600 766 0000 / 600 778 0000

Qleane

QLEANERS.COM
VICTOR@QLEANERS.COM

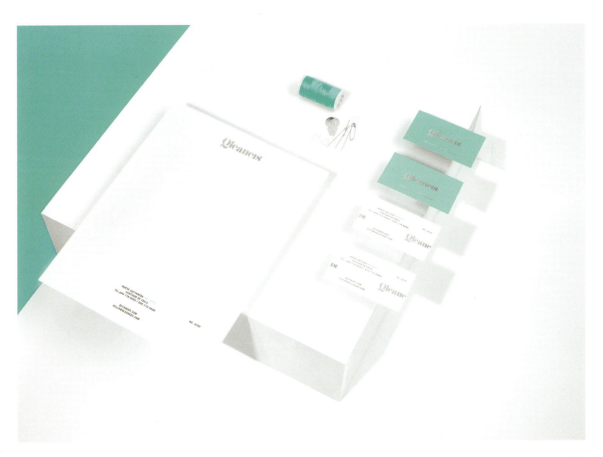

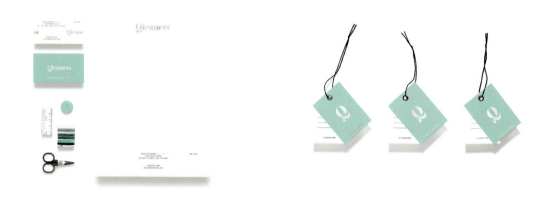

Viani

Design Agency: Moodley Brand Identity

Project Manager & Copywriter: Martin Zolles, Sabine Mühlwanger, Alexander Rehm

Art Director: Nora Obergeschwandner

Designer: Nora Obergeschwandner, Carolina Poch

Photography: Christoph Abatzis

Digital Design: Phil Samhaber

Client: Viani

Antonio Viani continued the family tradition of travelling the oceans to trade food in all corners of the world. This is how the former truffles shop became a place for delicacies. Viani only chooses the best goods for its range of products. To make this dedication also tangible in the B2C-area was the main task in rebranding Viani. Now the Italian "Joie de vivre" and the passion for all the good things can not only be found in the welcoming language but also the design. The repositioning sharpened the profile of the traditional family business, that can finally concentrate on the essential thing again: the good taste.

Fonts: Bauer Bodoni; Archer; Brown

Typeface Styles: Serif; Sans-Serif

PEPPER-razzi

MOSTO
wanted!

SCHWARZER URWALD-
PFEFFER, BIO
LE SPECIALITÀ DI VIANI, ITALIEN
Dose
5150 · 50 g · € 4,01 ·
3,40 (ab 6 Stück)

MOSTO
ARGENTO
CALVI, LIGURIEN
Flasche
1118 · 500 ml · € 10,02 ·
9,45 (ab 6 Stück)

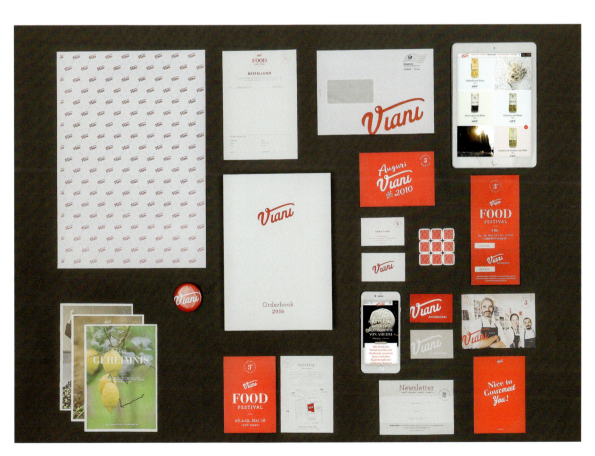

Centro Italia — Supermercato & Bistro

Project Manager & Copywriter: Emanuele Grifeo
Art Director: Nicholas Christowitz
Designer: Nicholas Christowitz
Client: Centro Italia

The designer was commissioned to update the visual identity of Centro Italia — Berlin's oldest and most loved Italian supermarket and bistro — to celebrate 50 years in business. Using classic wrought-iron Italian signage as a starting point, the designer created a logotype with character and confident restraint. The lockup functions as a classic mono-line logo while the holding device is a nod to the original signage of the store. The logo type was later expanded to additional posters, web navigation links, and signage.

**Original Logo
1968**

**Updated Logo
2018**

Fonts: Custom type; Gotham rounded
Typeface Styles: Sans-Serif

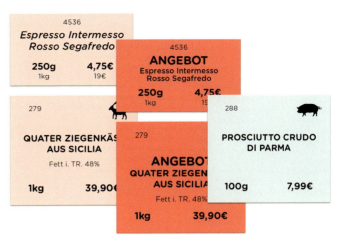

The Royale

Art Director: Nicholas Christowitz
Designer: Nicholas Christowitz
Client: Royale

The Designer was commissioned to create an identity for a Cuban-inspired bar and restaurant in Johannesburg, South Africa. The entire identity was created using The Royal Palm Hotel (in Havanna) as a starting point. An adaptable, custom font was created to allow for multiple variations across all collateral.

Fonts: Brown; Custom Logotype
Typeface Style: Sans-Serif

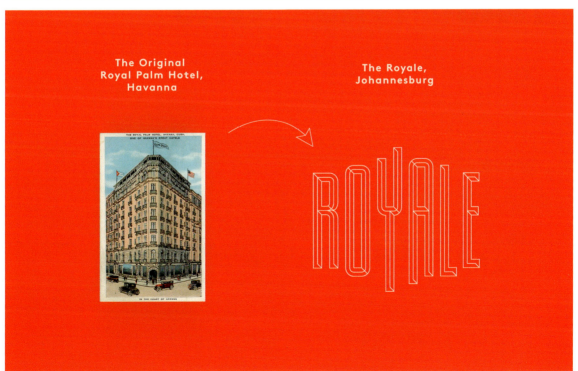

The Original
Royal Palm Hotel,
Havanna

The Royale,
Johannesburg

IVAJ

Design Agency: Nueve
Art Director: Nueve
Client: IVAJ

Designers were commissioned by the Generalitat Valenciana to renew the brand of the Institut Valencia de la Joventut (IVAJ). The IVAJ is the agency responsible of coordinating youth policy in the Valencian Community. Among the main functions of this agency are the defense of social rights and freedoms of young people, the promotion of youth participation and support for their structures, to prompt the provision of services for the youth, or to encourage educational leisure activities.

before

after

Font: Swiss 721
Typeface Style: Sans-Serif

The IVAJ needed a brand that would combine all the competencies of this organization, such as education in values, engagement, public service, and educational leisure, and also that would coexist with the rest of sub-brands of existing programs, such as Xarxa Jove, Viu, Tema Jove, and with the Generalitat Valenciana own brand.

For this, designers created a brand that would enhance and highlight the values for which the institution works. A purely typographical brand focused on the acronym IVAJ and inspired by sport as a symbol of positive values: participation, union, teamwork, integration, companionship, coexistence, cooperation, social responsibility, effort. An outright brand, in white and black, with a clear, direct typography and with a secondary colour range for graphic applications. Violet, orange and green complement the universe created for the institution. A purely typographical and colourful universe. The typeface used is Linotype's Swiss 721.

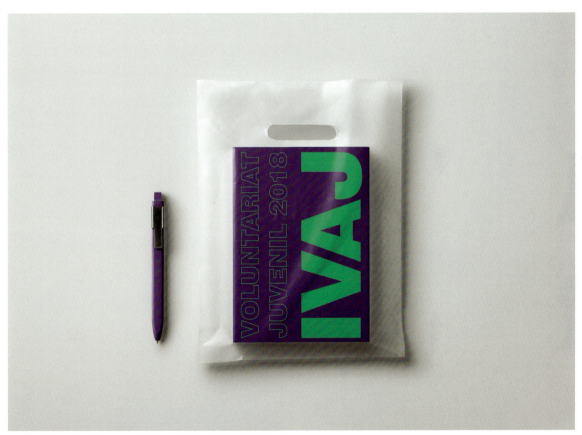

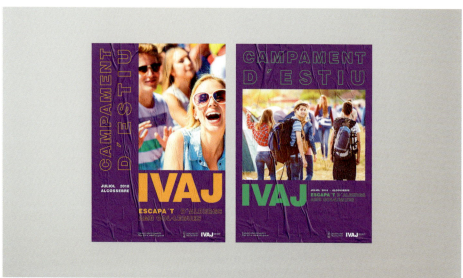

Dr. David Arévalo

Design Agency: Menta Picante
Creative Director: Alejandro Román, Gaby Salazar
Art Director: Alejandro Román
Client: Dr. David Arévalo

For this project the designer developed a graphic identity of an internist doctor, the commissioner wanted to communicate to his patients the security, tranquility and a detailed attention by being under a medical treatment, which is mostly made up of seniors who are concerned about taking care of their health.

In this graphic system, the designer has created an icon resembling the lymphatic system that happens to be one of the most important parts of the function of the human body. The stationary is simple with a grid framing the information to maintain the simplicity and the aesthetics of the project.

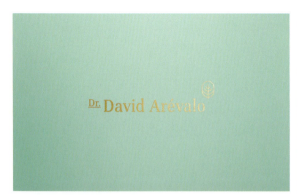
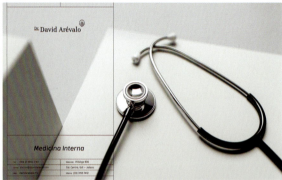

Font: Avila (Regular)
Typeface Style: Sans-Serif

Carpos

Design Agency: PANO DESIGN STUDIO
Designer: Panos Tsakiris
Creative Director: Panos Tsakiris
Artist: George Vavatsis
Photography: dt.Shoot
Client: Carpos

The studio was asked to design a system of products (a bottle and its packaging) that can safely hold the EVOO (Extra Virgin Olive Oil) par excellence. The main market is Switzerland where the company is also based. The chief aim was for the user to enjoy this experience with more than one senses and for this reason profound textures have been subtly incorporated in the design.

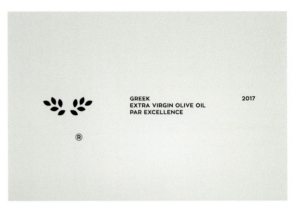

Font: Zona Pro
Typeface Style: Geometric Sans-Serif

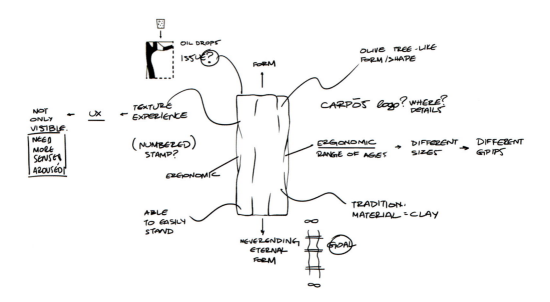

The inspiration for the solution has been mainly the form of the olive tree trunk in different ways and applications. The ethos of Carpos and the project's guidelines were the tools that 250 exclusively handcrafted bottles saw the light of the day. 750 olive trees in the mountains of Rhodope, Greece have been meticulously preserved throughout the year so that the user can enjoy this EVOO par excellence with care, like the way it was produced. Each of the 250 limited bottles is ready to be shipped individually in its own eco-sustainable packaging, structured with no adhesives. The minimalistic organic form of the bottle, the materials and its time-consuming process is what makes it look different. However, the attention to detail and love for what they do is what adds value to the brand.

Liv — Scandinavian Concept Store

Design Agency: Daniela Gilsdorf Graphic Design
Photography: Daniela Gilsdorf, Johannes Hermann
Client: Liv Hamburg

The corporate design for the concept store "Liv" in Hamburg was based on the clean and simple approach to design in Scandinavia. A unique bold font was custom made for Liv and is used for logo as well as headlines font. The "V" represents stylised trees and mountains of the Scandinavian countryside and forms the base of all patterns and elements. In order to integrate nature into the CI, everything was printed on recycled paper. Furthermore, opening hours were laser engraved into slices of birchwood, to tie along with the interior natural wood highlights. To contrast the calm black and white colour coding, neon orange was integrated to set a focal point.

THE QUICK BROWN FOX JUMPS OVER THE LAZY DOG?!

Ø123456789ÄÖÜÅÆØ:.!?€%.¨--

Liv — Scandinavian Concept Store 2

Design Agency: Daniela Gilsdorf Graphic Design
Production: Offset printing
Photography: Daniela Gilsdorf
Client: Liv Hamburg

A redesign of the Scandinavian concept store "Liv" in Hamburg. As part of an expansion, the brand is growing up while keeping the core values of a simple, clean design approach, tied to nature. Natural papers are used in combination with a characteristic marble pattern as the base. All-over prints are combined with outlined spaces that are in motion over the various print products. Aligning the custom made font in a bold way and integrating the heritage of the products by using Danish, Swedish and Norwegian headlines. Along with the base colours of black, white and marble a pop of naturally inspired colour range may be used. As a personal touch, the scrip font "Imogen Agnes" is used as an accent.

Fonts: The Store - Handset made by Daniela Gilsdorf; Futura
Typeface Styles: Sans-Serif (Petit Fou); Sans-Serif (Futura)

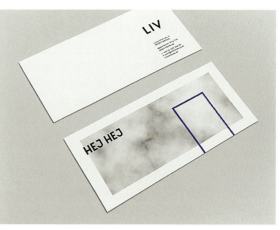

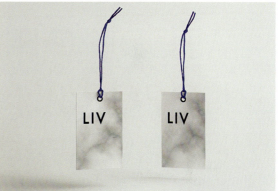

Petit Fou — Corporate Identity

Design Agency: Daniela Gilsdorf Graphic Design
Production: Digital printing, Laser cutting
Photography: Daniela Gilsdorf, Johannes Hermann
Client: Petit Fou

The concept of the corporate design is based on the brand name Petit Fou which translates as "Little Crazy One". As well as the product, the brand is young, fun and charming. The custom made font adapts the 45° angles from the clutches base structure and provides many quirky details. The logo follows a 9 point grid along every format and offers playful application possibilities. Pleasant details are included, for example the "Thank you": When the invoice is folded, it is the first thing to see when opening the envelope. The guiding thread is continued as far as the custom packaging, where the box is signed by each clutch artisan.

ABCDEFGHIJKLM
NOPQRSUTVWXYZ
0123456789
AOÜ.,„!?€&--

45° ANGLE EDGES   PLAYFUL DETAILS   UMLAUT MARKS

Fonts: Petit Fou - Handset made by Daniela Gilsdorf; Metric
Typeface Styles: Sans-Serif (Petit Fou); Sans-Serif (Metric)

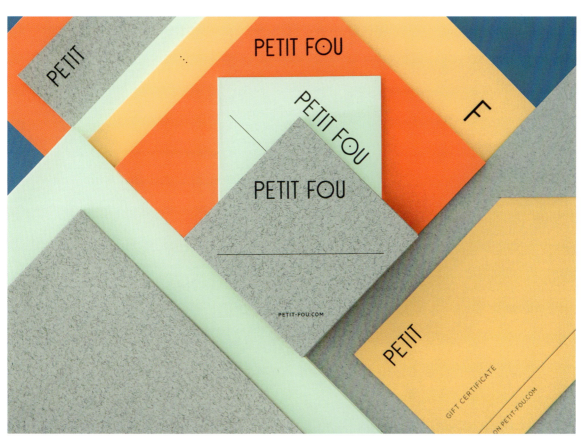

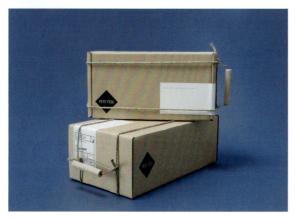

The 49th Golden Camera Awards — All about Yves

Creative Direction: Max Kuehne

Art Direction / Concept: Daniela Gilsdorf

Production: Relief-cut hot foil and hot foil embossing, Blind embossing, Offset and pigment silkscreen printing, Die cutting, Bookbinding, Water jet cutting

Photography: Daniela Gilsdorf, Johannes Hermann

Client: The Golden Camera Awards

The colour "Yves Klein Blue" builds the bold base for the modern French bistro approach of this event communication. To recreate the specific blue, a colour made of pigments was developed. The use of geometric forms and the resulting font created for the event are contrasted by the charming and detailed integration of patterns and illustrations in the overall design. The book-binded invitation with its double gate fold contains polished chrome as mirror for the use of the included phenakistiscope. The illustration on the phenakistiscope shows the "Golden Camera Trophy" in the flashlights of the red carpet. All stamps are entirely hot foil embossed.

Fonts: No. 49 - Handset made by Daniela Gilsdorf; Didot; News Gothic BT
Typeface Styles: Sans-Serif (No.49); Serif (Didot); Sans-Serif (News Gothic BT)

ABCDEF
GHIJKLM
NOPQRSTU
VWXYZ
ÄÖÜ

.,:; !?&-
0123456789

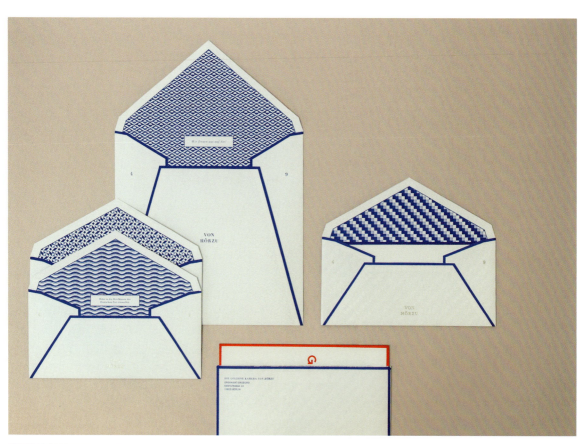

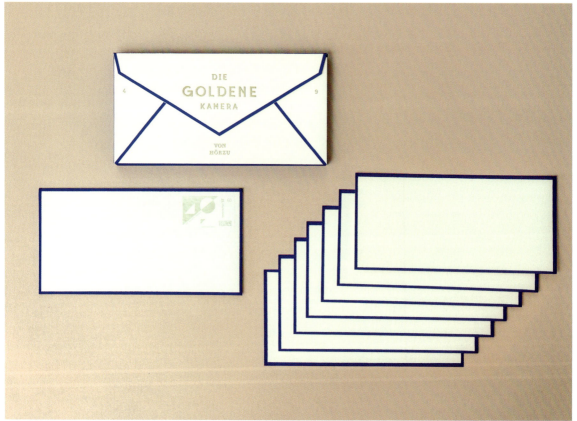

Eliza Branding

Design Agency: EME Design Studio
Project Manager & Copywriter: Enrique Avalos
Art Director: Joel Martinez, Iris Morales
Designer: Enrique Avalos
Illustrator: Enrique Avalos
Client: Eliza

Eliza is a hot metal bistro with a past that can't be forgotten, which is why every piece of the branding revolves around the J&L Steel Mill and the Eliza smokestack — the restaurant's namesake. Everything from the menu to the coasters has pieces alluding to the history of the region: with letters that come together like steel being assembled and numbers that reference the steel mill's past.

The designer wanted something simple and bold to complement the abstract and handmade deconstructed letters. The stars of the brand are the deconstructed letters that spell out the bistro's name. These letters use various layers, each one embellished with a different pattern or shade, to illustrate the parts of the letters coming together like several steel sheets. The additional elements of the nails, led to the steel with dashed lines, add to the illusion that these letters are truly in construction. Some sections of these split letters are accompanied by an encircled number, mimicking elements found in construction manuals.

Fonts: Gotham; Hand made font
Typeface Styles: Sans-Serif; Script

Hillside Branding

Design Agency: EME Design Studio
Project Manager & Copywriter: Boni Soto
Art Director: Joel Martinez, Iris Morales
Designer: Boni Soto, Enrique Avalos
Illustrator: Boni Soto, Enrique Avalos
Client: Hillside Coffee & Donut

Whether you're looking for a cup of delicious coffee or a twelve pack of donuts, you can make that experience one full of elegance and luxury by enveloping yourself in Hillside's branding. Every gold dot and line carefully placed by the designers at EME Design Studio makes grabbing a cup of coffee at Hillside an exquisite and memorable experience.

The project is ongoing and has to change from a coffee bag to a mug, to new cups. As designers realize that this brand keeps going, they have to be able to give themselves a chance to expand from what they began with. This is the reason they have used so many different fonts. It helps them to be more dynamic with each new piece. The challenge has been to find typefaces that work with the brand. The logo, a silhouette of the hillside enclosed in typography and a circle, punctuates every visual sentence.

To elaborate on Hillside's logo, the handcrafted typography used emphasizes the artisanal qualities of this coffee house. The mountains fill the logo halfway, symbolizing two different things. Firstly, Hillside is a local business located in El Paso, Texas, a place famous for its mountains. The fact that the mountains fill the circle halfway represents a coffee cup.

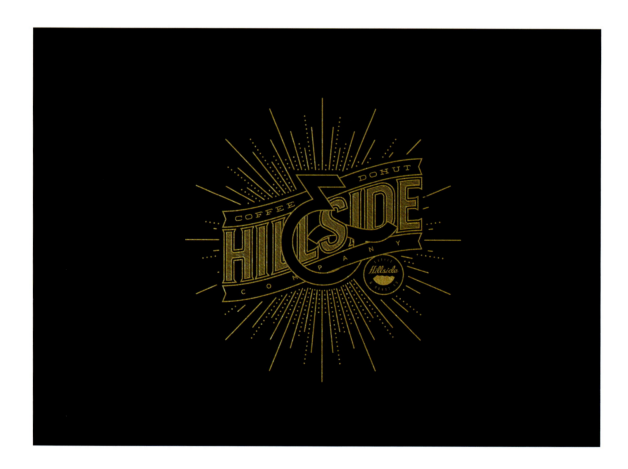

Fonts: Idaho; Gotham; Citizen Slab; Geared Slab; Antler; Appleton
Typeface Styles: Serif; Sans-Serif; Script; Slab Serif

The elements found on Hillside's packaging were all inspired by the vintage art deco style. Born from the desire to make everyday items beautiful, the mentality of the original style stays true here. For the most part, coffee cups and donut boxes are everyday items. However, given the Hillside touch, they have become elegant objects that allow the vigorous coffee drinker to experience luxury every morning.

The Upsider NYC

Design Agency: IWANT design
Art Director: John Gilsenan
Designer: John Gilsenan
Client: The Upsider

The Upsider is a restaurant on New Yorks Upper Eastside (Upsider). Working closely with Zachary Lynd, and to an extremely tight schedule, designers created a visual identity based around a suite of quirky illustrations, patterns and hand drawn type that riffed on the restaurant's name. The assets and colour palette were used subtly throughout the restaurant's interior, marketing and website to ensure that the naive quirky nature of the visual identity and the stylish interiors and food were perfectly balanced.

Designers wanted to create a naive handwritten font that would have a lot of personality, be flexible and have impact. They then used two supporting typefaces heavily kerned to create a modern retro feel.

Fonts: A bespoke naive hand-drawn typeface; Impact; Domaine Display Narrow
Typeface Styles: Sans-Serif; Script

Onery Brand Identity Design

Project Manager & Copywriter: Vinay Gowtham M
Designer: Vinay Gowtham M
Illustrator: Vinay Gowtham M
Client: Neha Aghara

Onery — Best Never Lies. It's a ceramic manufacturing company, floor and wall tiles. Onery product is quite different from others. Their produce tiles are just 3mm thick, which no one in India can make right now construction.

Typeface plays a major role in the iconic design. Designer always chooses the typeface based on the industry. Since Onery Brand is part of a manufacturing industry, so products will be very clean, as strong (indoor) and also as rough (outdoor and fashionable). Therefore, the designer has chosen the "Archive" Typeface. It has round soft corners and bold and strong style, which reminds people of small tiles.

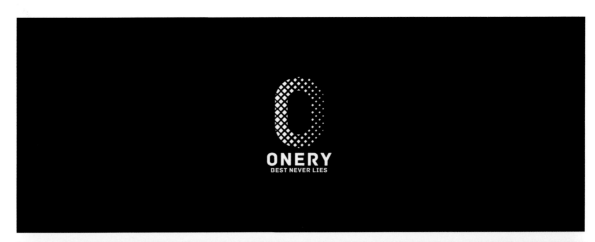

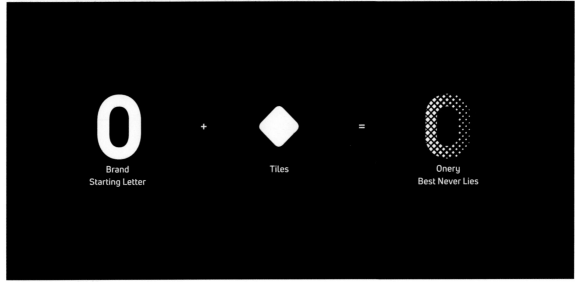

Fonts: Archive; UniNeue
Typeface Style: Sans-Serif

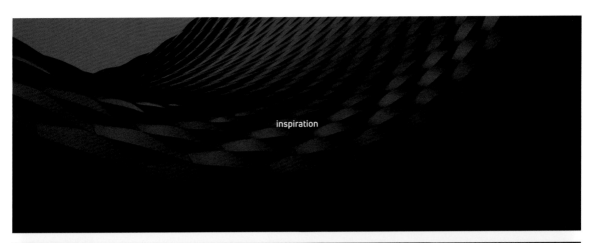

inspiration

BEST
NEVER LIES

ONERY

ARCHIVE FONT

**ARCHIVE BOLD FONT ARE
USED FOR BRAND NAME.**

A B C D E F G H I J
K L M N O P Q R S
T U V W X Y Z

1 2 3 4 5 6 7 8 9 0
! ? " " ' ' ( ) [ ] $ %
& / | @

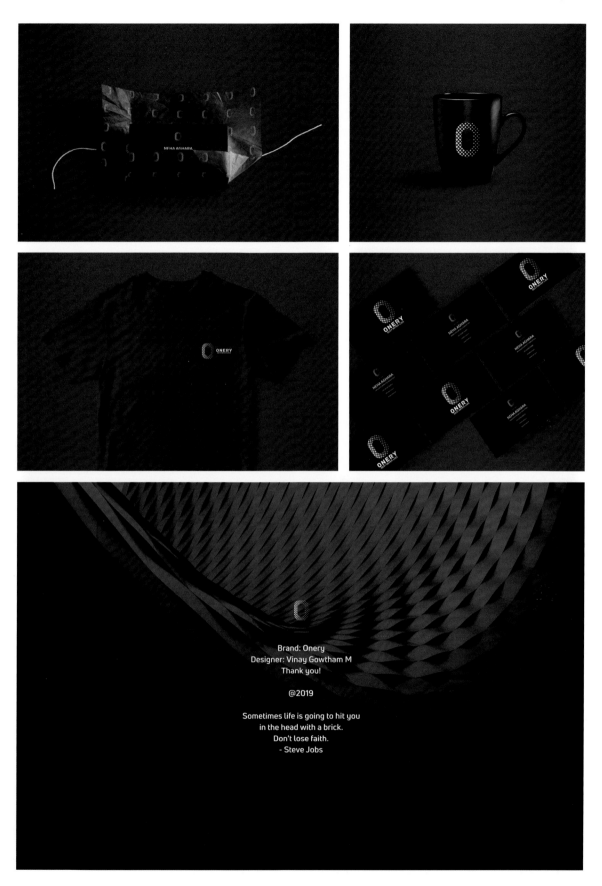

Brand: Onery
Designer: Vinay Gowtham M
Thank you!

@2019

Sometimes life is going to hit you
in the head with a brick.
Don't lose faith.
- Steve Jobs

Dumbo Burger

Design Agency: Solid Studio
Client: Dumbo

Dumbo is a small 24-seat pub based in Milan. They serve Burger, Lobster Roll and Salads, combined with a great selection of beers and first-class wines. Designers choose different fonts because they want to create font composition for printing, like poster, packaging, paper bags etc. The reflected initials and the vertical naming are details that turn the naming DUMBO in a burger. The "D" and the "O" are transformed into a bun that contains always different elements of the identity.

Fonts: Orator; Selima; Showcase; Swistblnk Banthers; Wisdom Script
Typeface Styles: Serif; Sans-Serif; Italic; Script; Fancy

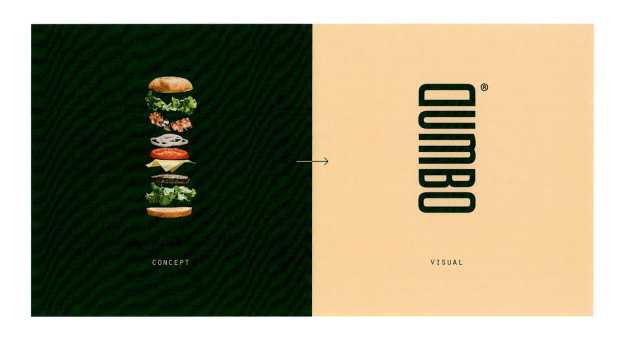

CONCEPT

VISUAL

Despensa N6 — Healthy Pastry

Design Agency: Savvy Agency
Project Manager & Copywriter: Joana Seixas
Art Director: Diogo Figueiredo
Designer: Francisco Malvar
Client: Despensa N6

Despensa N6 is a healthy pastry. Their products are 100% gluten free, 100% sugar free, and mostly of biological origin and lactose free. The branding proposal is inspired by the nutritional tables, which symbolizes the transparency of the product to the consumer. Designers created a pattern system inspired by sliced cakes, their layers, and also by the diversity of products that can be found in Despensa N6.

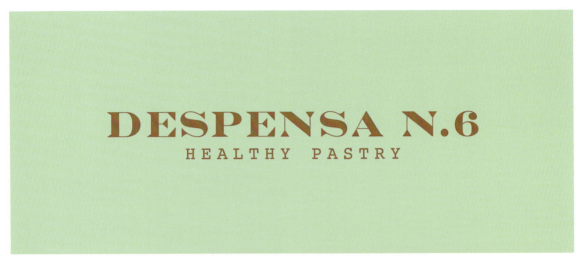

Fonts: Engravers; Courier
Typeface Styles: Serif; Slab Serif

For the main typeface, designers wanted to achieve a brand with great personality, without losing the unique side and elegant approach. In the description with wanted the simple, and yet honest side of the brand. In this project the typography had to be unique and timeless because the client didn't want a logomark, so the typography had to be exclusive.

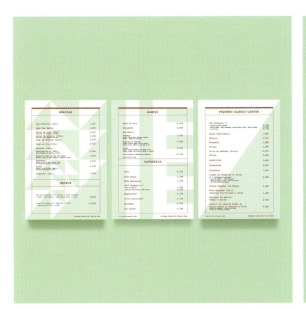

Sunny Dry Chips

Design Agency: Hi! Estudio
Project Manager & Copywriter: Gabriel Cuevas
Art Director: Gabriel Cuevas, Alan Aguiñaga
Designer: Gabriel Cuevas, Alan Aguiñaga
Photography: Alan Aguiñaga
Client: Kathia Vargas Montaño

A healthy homemade snack made from a selection of dehydrated fruits and vegetables baked as an alternative to industrialized potato chips.

The sunsets, dawns, a healthy lifestyle, the smile of people day after day, were trigger factors for the creation of the brand. A mark of friendly character plays with elements of colour for the differentiation of each one of the products. It is intended to communicate and promote through each of the applications that healthy eating can be simple and favorable for everyone.

Font: League Gothic
Typeface Style: Script

Naming
Sunny Dry Chips — It makes a direct reference to the sun, or sunny days that remind us how necessary they are for fruits and vegetables to grow naturally. The sun as a representative element of nature and the earth.

Logo
A composition was made where the main element is the Sunny word traced with rounded vertices, on the top five lines were placed radially in representation of the sun as a visual reinforcer of the name.

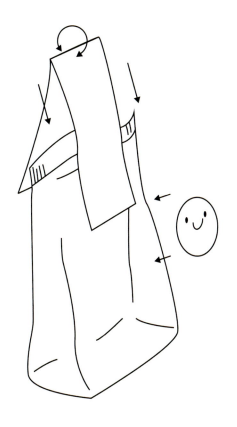

Visual Identity of Japanese brand "Man Qi Wu"

Design Agency: Do° Visual
Art Director: Gu Long

The brand name "Man Qi Wu" (鰻岐屋) means "House of Eel" in Japanese, so designers designed the logo in a lovely and interesting way, as fish in the lower part, with house roof above. The whole logo reminds people of the shape of the character " 食 " which means "food" and "eat" in English. Such logo also reflects the nature of restaurant. The suite of collateral is fun and elegant, and shows perfectly the charm of design and quality.

Also, the font has been designed in a light handwriting style, matching with the brand personality and the form of logo.

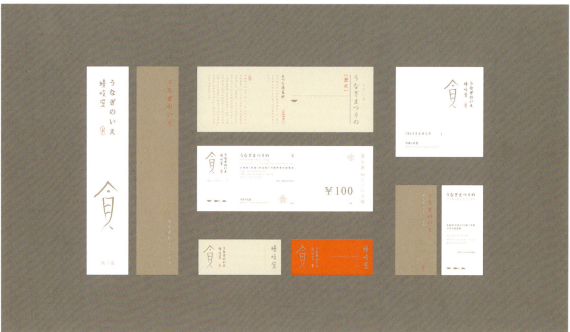

Fonts: Huakang Ming Dynasty (Japanese); Custom Font (Chinese)
Typeface Style: SimSun

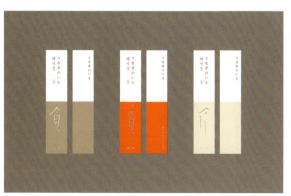

Noroshi

Design Agency: Mortise Design
Project Manager & Copywriter: Lee Ching Tat
Art Director: Lee Ching Tat
Designer: Lee Ching Tat
Illustrator: Lee Ching Tat
Photography: Lee Ching Tat
Client: Kojima Takatoshi

Noroshi is a Japanese ramen restaurant from Hakodate, serving regional noodle dishes since 2014. Hakodate is famous of its rich aquatic products. Noroshi would like to bring the indigenous flavour to Tokyo and the designer create a series of designs referring to that idea to manifest the property and origin of each ingredient. The Japanese characters のろし（Noroshi）means smoke signals which is illustrated by the graphic including the characters.

Font: Qingliu Clerical Script SIMO2_O
Typeface Style: Handwriting

のろしの特製香り味噌ダレ

四種類の
北海道の
赤味噌、白味噌

味噌

数種類の
特製スパイ
スと香味野
菜

オリジナルに
ブレンド、一週
間熟成させる

ダレ

深みのある
味わいとなっ
ています。

のろしのこだわりの塩ダレ

ミネラル豊富な
6種の海塩をオ
リジナルブレン

塩

北海道七飯町の
南横津岳の伏流
水を使い

ダレ

北海道産ホタテ
とあさり、最高
級昆布から海鮮
の出汁をたっぷり
と

のろし特製香り
チャーシュー丼

厳選したハブ肉を、長時間スパイス、
香味野菜と煮ることにより、
豚の臭みが消えより柔らかくなり自家特製辛味ダレをいれ、
2段階の味入れによる旨みの向上。

お得　11：00〜15：00
ラーメンと一緒に購入する場合
200yen→150yen

Sakagura Cafe

Design Agency: Tegusu
Project Manager & Copywriter: Anchorman
Art Director: Masaomi Fujita
Designer: Masaomi Fujita
Photography: Yoshiro Hayakawa
Client: Iinuma Honke

Iinuma Honke is a sake brewery located in Shisui, Shiba Prefecture. On their property, there is a building called "Magariya". It used to be an old private house in Niigata Prefecture, but it was relocated and refurbished, and turned into a building used for selling sake, eating and drinking, and as a gallery. When they renewed the building to be reused as "Sakagura Cafe", Tegusu handled the overall production of work, including the development of the shop concept and print media such as the symbol logo, leaflet, poster and menu, and the design of items like mugs and paper cups for takeout.

Fonts: Copperplate Regular (English); Original (Japanese)
Typeface Style: Serif (English)

The concept of Sakagura Cafe is represented in the symbol logo, in which you can see an icon of a brewer working beside a sake storage tank disguised as a mug. It also has motifs of rice fields and stocks of rice, the blessings of nature. Indigo dyed noren (a split short curtain) is used in the main graphic piece and it appears in many items. This gives these items a Japanese taste and a unified impression.

Senseu Atelier

Design Agency: Siwei Design
Project Manager & Copywriter: Lai Siwei
Art Director: Lai Siwei
Designer: Lai Siwei
Client: Senseu Atelier

The designer didn't position this project in a specific style at first hand, instead, they preferred to express the brand in an abstract way, with plenty of details in the work. The logo is formed in calligraphic strokes expressed in a Chinese old saying "Starting as silkworm head, and finishing as swallow tail."[1] The form in different colours were used to contrast with strokes, adding modern style to the whole identity. The visual design shaped the specific personality of Senseu Atelier, balancing between realism and abstractionism.

Fonts: Custom font for "SU"; Bordofixed Tryout as auxiliary font
Typeface Style: Serif

1 Starting as silkworm head, and finishing as swallow tail: Chinese saying describing a Calligraphic style. Calligrapher starts the character in strong stroke, and finishes in a light and fast manner. When writing a stroke in the style of Han Dynasty, it's recommended to set back a bit the stroke in both starting and finishing point. The shape of backstroke in starting point should be as silkworm head, and when finished, it should be similar to swallow tail.

little tea house

Art Director: Anthony Au Yeung
Designer: Anthony Au Yeung

Little tea house is not a commercial project, but the designer's private practice. The idea is to tell a story about destiny: It rained in a sudden, a lady and a gentleman met up with each other in a little tea house when they looked for shelter from the rain. When the sky cleared up, the two left together with an open ending. Falling in love with each other is the result of luck; however, the destiny finally unites lovers in marriage. Destiny is never predictable, hence, we should appreciate the luck which makes us meet each other, cherish the destiny which unites us together, and remember the happiness of life as we often enjoy the enduring fragrance of tea.

The little tea house plays the role as bartender in a pub, or a bystander in your life. It witnesses people meeting up each other by destiny.

Font: Custom; 筑紫 A 丸ゴシック
Typeface Style: Sans-Serifs

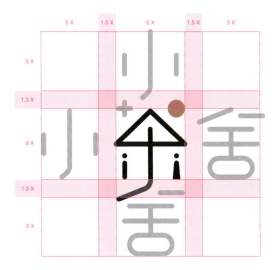

The horns of characters in the style of calligraphy, handwriting or boldface deliver too much emotion. So the designer chose rounded typeface, which is consistent in stroke with round finishes, to express a gentle and stable atmosphere.

The layout is simple: Proper white space not only avoids too much emotion, but also leaves more space for people to image. Moreover, the first letters of "little tea house" are all in lower-case, which reinforces the nature of little in brand name.

Enchantée

Design Agency: Triangler Studio
Project Manager & Copywriter: Chi-Yao Tang
Art Director: Chun-Yao Huang
Designer: Hsiang-Chia Wu, Yi Wang
Illustrator: Chun-Yao Huang
Photography: Chi-Yao Tang
Client: Enchantée

Enchantée is a new handmade French dessert brand targeting on wedding gift boxes market. The brand spirit of happiness and elegance are expressed through the bright colours and the logo of a dancing lady. The lady who wears a french style hat is dancing not only for the upcoming wedding but also for the tastiness of the desserts. Her tutu skirt mixes the shape of the classic French madeleine. Bodoni Book is the classic font for the logotype to show the cultural feeling and the elegance of the brand. A consistent of softness is perceptible whenever browsing the website online or receiving the tangible prints and packing boxes.

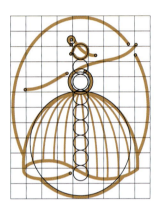

楽 朗 奇

enchantée

Bodoni Std   ABCDEFGHIJKLMNOPQRSTUVWXYZ
abcdefghijklmnopqrstuvwxyz

Fonts: Bodoni Book; Avenir; Source Han Serif
Typeface Styles: Serif; Sans-Serif

Premium
Venetian Red

Classic

經典悅人

Classic

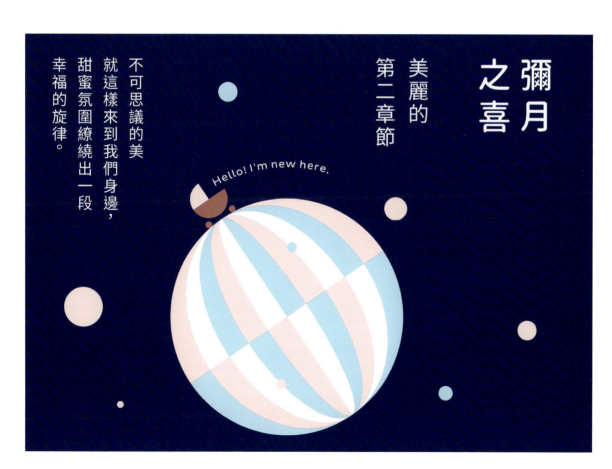

彌月之喜

美麗的
第二章節

不可思議的美
就這樣來到我們身邊，
甜蜜氛圍繚繞出一段
幸福的旋律。

Hello! I'm new here.

Let's Freeze Your Spirit

Design Agency: Parklane by Splender
Project Manager & Copywriter:
Parklane by Splender
Art Director: Huang Zhongxing
Designer: Huang Zhongxing
Client: Parklane by Splender

Let's Freeze Your Spirit, for the project to design visual identity of a store, designers wanted to make clients feel more comfortable on the scorcher. They chose the font with casual stroke, integrating with colour code which make people feel cool, and the transparent materials, to convey the impression of fresh and pleasant during summer days.

Font: Blair
Typeface Style: Sans-Serif

開張
作伙
歡迎

天越熱
心要越涼
越熱越涼

LETS FREEZE
YOUR SPIRIT
2018
SUMMER

宅家涼
HOME
STUFF

穿得涼
CLOTHING
ACCESSORIES

雨來涼
RAIN
STUFF

肌淨涼
SKIN
PRODUCTS

呷涼舖
TAIWAN TRADITIONAL
ICE

讓身體
納涼
CHILL
&
TASTE

歡作開
迎伙張

Macao Doulao

Design Agency: Perfect Design
Project Manager & Copywriter: Chen Guanyu, David
Art Director: Chen Guanyu
Designer: Xue Wenxin
Client: Macao Doulao

The Chinese name of Doulao is the transliteration of English word "Dollar", and Chinese pronounce it similar to the phrase "gain together" which implies people's wish to gain happiness, fortune and luck. Macao Doulao includes high-quality ingredients from all over the world. The traditional hotpot soup cooked in secret recipe was upgraded by modern technology, resulting to the iconic hotpot culture with special urban characteristics.

Designers started the brand redesigning by upgrading the logo. The original heavy structure was re-organized to flatten it visually. Creative icon of postmark shows the effort of the brand to deliver hotpot food from the other side of the sea. When refining the visual signage in posters and packaging, designers selected the elements from Hong Kong culture, the illustration style and the colour palette in contrast to reinforce clients' memory to the brand name. Also, the designer constructed the advertising copy in the popular style which could attract young people and increase the readability of the text.

Current typefaces highlight Hong Kong cultural style, reinforces people's understanding of the brand, and differentiate it from other similar Macao hotpot brands on the market. In typography, the grid system leads people's visual focus. Different paragraphs were classified and placed in different sections according to the logic of visual focus.

 × ×

Fonts: Calligraphic font; Retro font
Typeface Styles: Serif; Italic

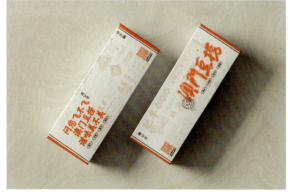

Mukden Skewers

Design Agency: Perfect Design
Project Manager & Copywriter: Chen Guanyu
Art Director: Chen Guanyu
Designer: Chen Guanyu, Liu Bo
Client: Mukden Skewers

Mukden Skewers is a very distinctive and creative brand located in Tiexi District of Shenyang, targeting young clients between 20 and 35 years old. Mukden is the ancient name of Shenyang, which used to be a key city for heavy industry, with profound cultural background. The typeface was designed in a rough style to express the sense of power, matching up with the theme of the project. In the meantime, a series of creative product not only makes the brand more interesting, but also provides clients with a sense of participation. And these are the brand's intellectual property (IP) which fits the taste of young people.

Font: Calligraphic font
Typeface Styles: Serif; Others

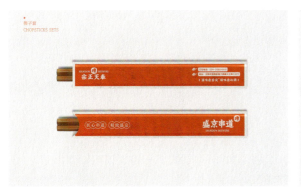

筷子套
CHOPSTICKS SETS

名片
BUSINESS CARD

饮品杯
DRINKS CUP

衍生品T恤（服装类）
TEE

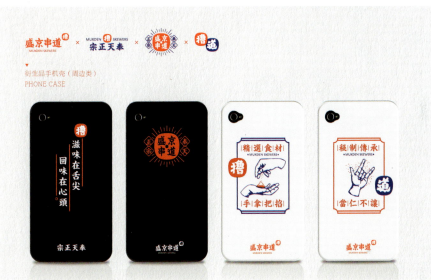

衍生品手机壳（周边类）
PHONE CASE

■ PEREFECT DESIGN 极好品牌整合设计　　　■ Profile　　　■ 简要介绍

工作服（服装类）
WORK CLOTHES

She Why Izakaya

Design Agency: Shinsun

She Why comes from Chinese idioms "Keep out of the affair", which means to put oneself outside of things and give the mind a place to rest. "She why" is a British-style izakaya opened in China. The owner has returned to China after living in the UK for many years and she hopes to bring the culture of British izakaya to the Chinese people. "I hope to provide a place where people can let go of their worries, unhappiness and distractions after their daily work, and put their bodies in 'out of the way' to give their minds a place to rest," she says.

The heart is in "She why", and happiness is in it. This slogan is about resting the mind, letting go of obsessions and feeling free.

BRITISH IZAKAYA 英式居酒屋

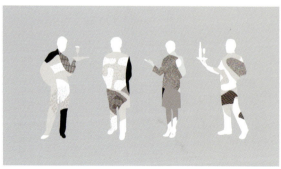

Font: Custom-made
Typeface Styles: Script; Serif

Chinese calligraphy advocates 'clumsiness', a simplicity of brushwork and a lovely authenticity that is in keeping with the spontaneous tone of the 'She why' approach. This is why the Chinese calligraphic characters were chosen as the expressive element of the logo. At the same time, the designers have worked on the details to make the typeface look like a slightly drunken person. The irregular borders of the typeface resemble the staggering steps of a person who has been drinking, in order to convey the hazy, beautiful, spontaneous and free nature of the brand.

Lacoco Cafe

Design Agency: Akronim
Project Manager: Anas Kautsar
Art Director / Design Director: Adji Herdanto
Designers: Adji Herdanto, Anas Kautsar
Photography: Anas Kautsar
Client: Lacoco Cafe

Branding and visual identity design for Lacoco, a Cafe and meet-up-hub located in East Jakarta, Indonesia. This Cafe was started as a place to drink coconut, stated in their previous name "La Coco" which means coconut. As the business grows, they start to sell other products and create the cafe mood more general. So designers help them to rejuvenate their brand by changing the name first from "La Coco" into "Lacoco Cafe" as they not only sell coconut, but also specialty coffee and other food and beverages.

The identity is designed to look simpler and less graphic to support the overall brand positioning. Main symbol of Lacoco logo created from the consonant letter of the brand name, which is spelled into LCC. It will help the name to be recognised easily by the audiences and also creating a brand symbol that have a strong characteristic which they have not had before.

Colour Scheme

Primary

C0 M35 Y85 K0
R251 G176 B64

Secondary

C0 M0 Y0 K100
R0 G0 B0
#000000

Neutral Colour

C0 M0 Y0 K0
R255 G255 B255
#FFFFFF

Logo in Grid / Diagram

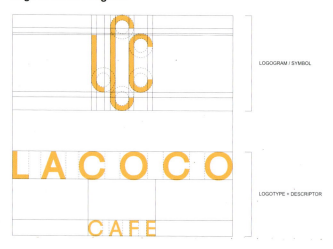

LOGOGRAM / SYMBOL

LOGOTYPE + DESCRIPTOR

Fonts used: Neuzeit S (Logotype); Avenir (Corporate Typeface)
Typeface Style: Sans-Serif

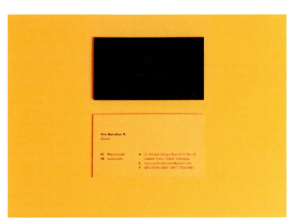

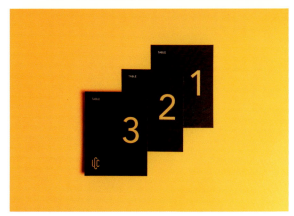

Jane K

Designer: Elena Simonova
Client: Jane K

Jane K is a new Russian brand of women's clothing, modern, laconic and very feminine. The target audience is young women from 23 to 35 with higher education, actively interested in art, creativity and travel. They want to combine comfort and feminine silhouettes, pay attention to quality and fabric. Based on the brief, the brand concept was proposed in pastel shades. The colour scheme inspired by the collection and the simplicity of design emphasizes the refinement and style of the brand. A strict and feminine image of the brand was created. The project has received a lot of feedback and positive comments.

Colour Scheme

Primary

C22 M53 Y44 K0
R198 G133 B127

C0 M13 Y18 K0
R247 G222 B202

C60 M61 Y44 K46
R75 G66 B61

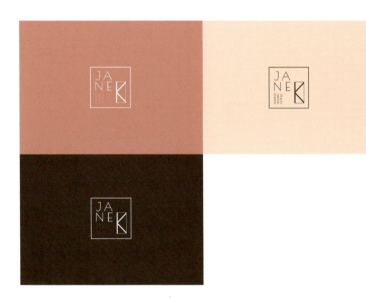

Logo in Grid / Diagram

Fonts used: Poiret One; Myriad Pro
Typeface Style: Sans-Serif

Henricus – Fermenterij van Dam

Design Agency: Super Silo
Project Manager & Copywriter: Martijn van Dam
Photography: Martijn van Dam
Illustrator: Martijn van Dam
Client: Fermenterij van Dam

Fermenterij van Dam is a home brewery from the province of Brabant in the South of the Netherlands, founded by designer Martijn's brother Rik. For the label design Martijn created an elaborate illustration based around a hop-inspired character that contains a lot of references to the authentic brewing process. The fonts used in the design are from the Knockout and Proxima Nova font families. Clean Sans-Serif fonts that work nicely with the understated appearance of the label. The name of the beer "Henricus" is build up using an edited Knockout Condensed font and stylised by enlarging the first and last letter. A golden sticker is placed on top of the paper labels to define the type of beer. The choice of materials, hand-application of the labels and details within the illustration reflect the nature of the beer: a true labour of love.

Colour Scheme

Primary

C0 M3 Y10 K10

C0 M5 Y15 K35

Secondary

C30 M30 Y50 K100

C0 M0 Y0 K0

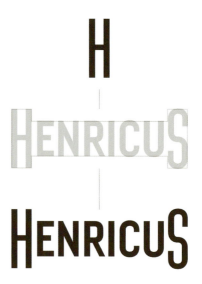

Logo in Grid / Diagram

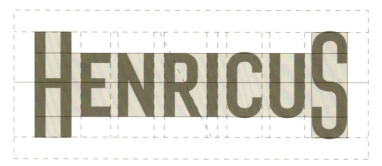

Fonts used: Knockout; HTF29 Junior Lite weight; HTF32 Junior Cruiser weight
Typeface Style: Sans-Serif

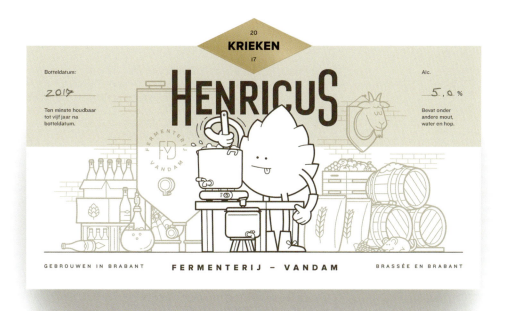

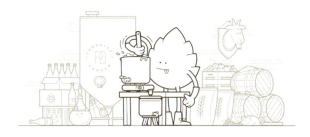

Soo Zee 23

Design Agency: The Creative Method
Project Manager & Copywriter: Tony Ibbotson, Lee Nicol
Art Director: Tony Ibbotson
Designer: Emma Lucia
Client: Chatime

Soo Zee 23's broth is handcrafted using a blend of 23 herbs and spices in an 8 hour process. Using only the freshest ingredients, the result is authentic and tasty beef noodle soup. "Soo Zee" is Sichuanese for "number", and "23" represents the number of blended herbs and spices used to create their famous broth. Chinese characters for "eat" (吃) and "23" (二三) feature in the identity to echo the theme of cuisine brand.

A crafted typeface was created for the logo, combining three languages including dialects together (Mandarin, Sichuanese and English). The typography provides a deliberate contrast between the graphics, a contemporary logo mark paired with traditional imagery. This reinforces the idea of authentic dining in a modern setting. The lines of " 二三 " (23) seen in the logo reflect how the images work together in a horizontal and vertically sliced format across the entire brand.

The logo idea of Soo Zee 23 came from the unique product story. The company's core product offering was an authentic spicy broth containing 23 unique ingredients. The colours used in font were taken from a hero product image distilling lighter and darker shades of the spicy broth. The contrast had to be enough to enable the characters " 二三 " (23) to show but also enable the logo to be viewed as a whole.

Colour Scheme

Primary

R235 G95 B59
Pantone 2013

R255 G152 B0
Pantone 2027

Logo in Grid / Diagram

Font used: Bebas Neue
Typeface Styles: Sans-Serif; Custom

Rb5 Vinícola

Design Agency: Victor Weiss Design
Project Manager & Copywriter: Victor Weiss
Art Director: Victor Weiss
Designer: Victor Weiss
Client: João Vitor Bartolini

The Rb5, began in 1853, is a winery located in a region of Italian colonization, with the devotion of the five Bartolini brothers. The brand is characterised by a combination of quality, tradition and technological innovation, which the designer wanted to convey.

The logo was a monogram, on plain view the icon that seems to be a sophisticated number 5, but it has the "r" and the "b" as well. As the secondary concept, designer added the drops on the far ends, and in the negative space a whine opener. Designer chose Evergreen and Inkland fonts because they were the perfect combination between sophistication and artistic. Evergreen is a clean sophisticated, very well elaborated font. It is used for the companies' name and ad titles. Inkland is very artistic and delicate typography. It has this "ink" look that also reminds people of spilled whine, so that it is destined to the tagline. The designer also worked a little with the curves and details so it would fit better Rb5's visual brand. Normally most whine visual brands use typical serifs like Times New Roman, Trajan Pro, Caslon, Garamond etc., but designer not only wanted to create something original, it had to be the perfect line between modern and antique, sophisticated and artistic, and that is always a challenge.

Colour Scheme

Primary

#221f1f

Secondary

C27 M90 Y63 K26
#992d3c

C31 M82 Y34 K21
#9c3f62

C10 M36 Y79 K1
#e6ab43

C13 M84 Y66 K3
#d14649

#e8e5e0

C10 M62 Y43 K1
#dd7b7a

Logo in Grid / Diagram

Fonts used: Evergreen; Inkland
Typeface Styles: Sans-Serif; Script

Asei Architects

Design Agency: Tegusu
Art Director: Masaomi Fujita
Designer: Masaomi Fujita
Client: Asei Architects

Asei Architects, a company based in Tokyo led by Mr. Asei Suzuki provide planning, design and management of architecture and interiors located throughout Japan. They deal with various kinds of architecture including residential buildings and cultural facilities with the vision of "empowering architecture", making people recapture the hidden charms of local areas or environment. Tegusu handled the VI and concept development for the company.

While the font is geometric and has a stout structure, it is created based on "Gotham," which is not too mechanical and has human-like softness. Designers got inspiration from the shape of " 亜 ", the kanji used in the company name "Asei", which is also Mr. Suzuki's first name, in visualizing Asei's philosophy and style.

Mint blue is a colour that is associated with natural things such as water and air, and it's arranged with black to make this subtle colour combination. They came up with the colour combination that is hard to describe with words to reflect a delicate impression "Kankyo", the word used in Asei's business theme.

Colour Scheme

Primary

C13 M0 Y6 K100

C0 M0 Y0 K0
R255 G255 B255
#FFFFFF

Secondary

C13 M0 Y6 K40

C13 M0 Y6 K0

Logo in Grid / Diagram

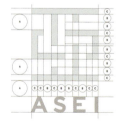

Typeface Style: Sans-Serif

Maldini Studios

Art Director: Jens Nilsson
Designer: Jens Nilsson
Photography: Jens Nilsson
Client: Maldini Studios

Identity for the Stockholm based interior design and carpenter firm Maldini Studios. The studio consists of a project manager and carpenter Rasmus Moberg, interior designer Elina Johansson and carpenter Theo Klyvare. The identity has a high focus on textures and materials with the custom made typeface, Donadoni, as the main component. The letterpress printed stationaries are printed on mixed textured papers from GF Smith and Arjowiggins.

Colour Scheme

Primary

C0 M0 Y0 K0
R255 G255 B255
#FFFFFF

C88 M53 Y65 K57
R23 G59 B48
#173b30

Logo in Grid / Diagram

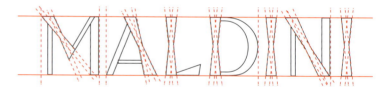

First Rejected Explorations

MALDINI   Maldini

MALDINI   MALDINI

MaLDINI   MALDINI

MALDINI

Fonts used: Futura; Donadoni (custom font for Maldini Studios)
Typeface Style: Sans-Serif

Alameda Shoes Concept Store

Design Agency: Bullseye
Client: Alameda

Alameda is a shoes concept store, with a wide range of products, currently markets more than 40 brands of ready-to-wear, footwear, fashion accessories, design and lifestyle, perfumes, gadgets and decoration. An innovative concept, a project that aims to provide a new shopping experience, presenting the latest national and international trends, through a careful selection of designers, with the presentation of high quality products and unique design.

A brand identity developed to communicate a store with high fashion goods, therefore designer have used twos colour tones resembling this refinement atmosphere. It's adapted typography design, has a geometric input communicating the brand's concept in style and elegance.

Colour Scheme

Primary

C80 M55 Y60 K50

Pantone 872U

Logo in Grid / Diagram

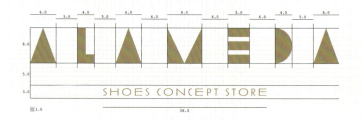

Fonts used: Custom; Anisette
Typeface Style: Sans-Serif

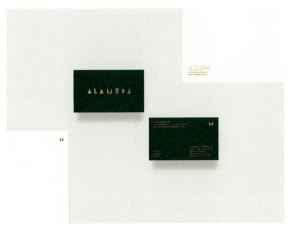

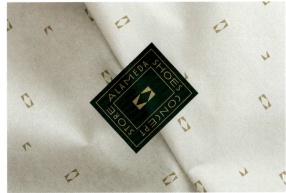

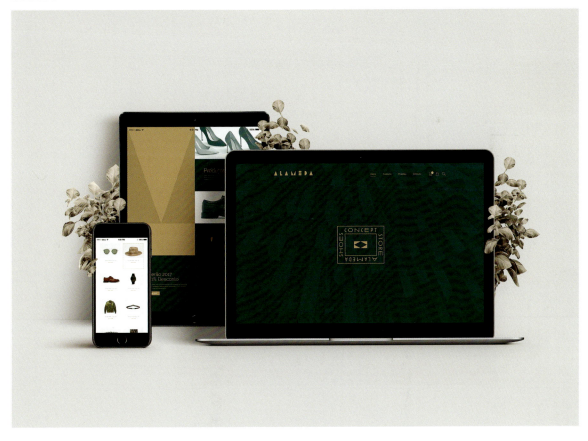

Mimo Kids Concept Store

Design Agency: Bullseye
Client: Mimo

Mimo Kids Concept Store, a space of new trends in a world full of trammels, play and passion for children's fashion. The new concept store with an identity that conveys all the purity and energy concentrated in the little ones.

In this project designer have used graphic elements that represent the playfulness of children, with a contemporary look. Also, they've design a packaging concept and the brand website with Mimo's identity. The brand has a bold logo typography symbolising the adventurous children side in pursuing their dreams. Communicating the children purity with stylish clothing like grown-ups, they've created a combination between style and adventure.

Colour Scheme

Primary

C100 M100 Y100 K100

Secondary

C20 M35 Y35 K10

C30 M15 Y15 K0

Logo in Grid / Diagram

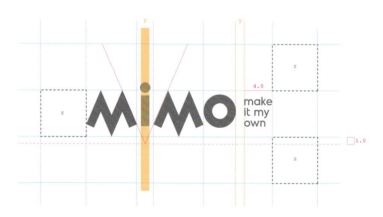

Fonts used: Varies; Odudo
Typeface Style: Sans-Serif

Grpl Green Platform

Design Agency: Form & Function
Project Manager & Copywriter: Chung, Jinsuh
Art Director: Chung, Jinsuh
Designer: Chung, Jinsuh
Client: Nara Hosticultral

Grpl is a plant sales brand that centres on a convenient system in which users can choose and purchase green plants to suit their tastes, along with a variety of pots. The logo of Grpl is a concept that visualises the process of plant growth that changes over and over again, resulting in the repetition and change of leaves designed by circles.

Helvetica Neue, used in Grpl, is a symbolic typeface of internationalism that conveys a neutral feeling. This typeface fits well with Grpl's brand image, which centres on rules, order and systems, and delivers images that do not change over a long period of time. In one medium, only one weight of typeface is used, and the layout uses asymmetrical formats that can express images of rules and changes.

Colour Scheme

Primary

C100 M0 Y100 K85
R0 G52 B7
Pantone 7484C

C40 M0 Y35 K0
R154 G211 B183
Pantone 571C

Logo in Grid / Diagram

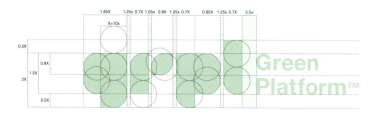

Font used: Helvetica Neue LT std
Typeface Style: Sans-Serif

Ideën

Design Agency: The Branding People
Client: Ideën

Ideën is a Dutch inspired brand based in Mexico that produces and distributes a wide range of commodities designed for modern life, offering smart living products. Designers created a sober and steady brand system inspired by Scandinavian design using all the different products as main elements for its communication. To avoid visual distractions they used a palette of neutral colours that let materials speak for themselves and to keep the brand from going too sober, they added orange and blue hints that perfectly play with textures and geometric shapes as they display the fun and innovative personality of the brand.

In order to express a "simple living" lifestyle, a set of clean, bold and overall Nordic typographies were chosen, this helped in creating big and descriptive messages throughout the brand's touching points. The set includes the Fago, Galano, Helvetica and Maison Neue fonts so they could work together and build a very technical layout that helped adding firmness and a sense of innovation into the packaging. This particular use of fonts helped designers develop a typographic system that is the back bone of the brand.

Colour Scheme

Primary

C55 M0 Y27 K0
Pantone 3242C

Secondary

C0 M50 Y95 K0
Pantone 1495C

C30 M20 Y20 K5
Pantone 421C

C10 M10 Y5 K0
Pantone 663C

Logo in Grid / Diagram

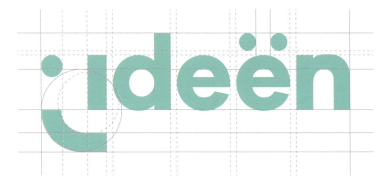

Fonts used: Fago; Galano; Helvetica; Maison
Typeface Styles: Sans-Serif; Slab Serif

Marmarina

Design Agency: Dmentes Estudio Creativo
Project Manager & Copywriter: Eva Canal Pesquera
Art Director: Eva Canal Pesquera
Designer: Eva Canal Pesquera
Illustrator: Eva Canal Pesquera
Client: Fenorgil S.L.

The logotype that makes up the brand comes from the Baskerville Classico Typeface. The modulation of his stroke remembers a classic writing and reflects elegance on his form. It's a typeface that evokes the times in which the fonts were created in an artisanal way for use in printing, like the illustration of the brand.

The name marmarina is a combination of the Spanish words "Mar" and "Marina". Linked with the pictorial technique of watercolor. For this reason the logo has an undulation that cut the characters in half simulating a wave.

Colour Scheme

Primary

C0 M0 Y0 K100
R28 G28 B27
Pantone P179-16U

Secondary

C100 M0 Y15 K60
R0 G84 B108
Pantone P120-16U

C0 M79 Y59 K0
R234 G83 B85
Pantone P55-6C

marmarina

invitaciones & detalles

Logo in Grid / Diagram

Font used: Baskerville Classic
Typeface Styles: Serif; Italic

Manitú

Design Agency: Dmentes Estudio Creativo
Project Manager & Copywriter: Eva Canal Pesquera
Art Director: Eva Canal Pesquera
Designer: Carlos González Iglesias
Illustrator: Eva Canal Pesquera
Client: Manitú

Manitú is a store of educational toys, whose name comes from the Great Spirit of the Canadian Algonquin tribes. Designers chose typography with great readability and uppercase, to facilitate reading to children. They also create a visual game of counter form inside the letter A, in which customers can see a tip that refers to the indigenous tribes and that will become a symbol of the brand. The Rubik typeface has been modified to round the vertex, giving it a kinder look. In addition, the generous thickness of the letters ensures that they do not lose prominence together with the illustrations, forming part of the compositions in a balanced way.

Colour Scheme

Primary

C6 M69 Y51 K0
R237 G109 B105
Pantone 55-5U
#ed6d69

C0 M57 Y42 K35
R176 G103 B96
Pantone 56-13U
#b06760

Secondary

C0 M19 Y43 K11
R232 G197 B147
Pantone 18-3U
#e8c593

C58 M0 Y31 K13
R100 G176 B171
Pantone 128-4U
#64b0ab

C31 M0 Y16 K0
R188 G224 B222
Pantone 127-2U
#bce0de

C0 M33 Y52 K26
R199 G152 B107
Pantone P 29-4U
#c7986b

C22 M31 Y34 K0
R207 G180 B165
Pantone 33-3U/30%
#cfb4a5

Logo in Grid / Diagram

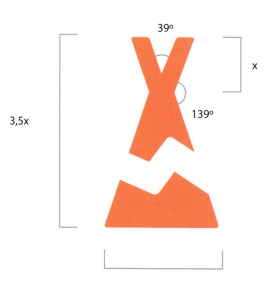

Font used: Rubik
Typeface Style: Sans-Serif

Konkovo Bookstore

Designer: Anastasia Kurilenko
Photography: Polina Sharai

This project is designed for a bookstore located in Moscow. The logo is made by merging a typographical glyph and an image of a seahorse. Why did designer use the seahorse in particular? Because if you read "Konkovo" in Russian, you might have noticed that the name consists of the word "horse"(конь). That's why she took the word as a basis, replacing it with a seahorse to make it look more like a section sign "§".

Colour Scheme

Primary

C3 M2 Y2 K0
R248 G248 B248
#F8F8F8

C27 M11 Y24 K2
R195 G207 B197
#C3CFC5

C7 M54 Y98 K33
R171 G104 B32
#AB6820

C95 M93 Y47 K95
R11 G11 B11
#0B0B0B

Logo in Grid / Diagram

Font used: Noto Serif Bold
Typeface Style: Serif

Joselo Café

Design Agency: Henriquez Lara Estudio
Project Manager & Copywriter: Javier Henríquez Lara
Art Director: Javier Henríquez Lara
Designer: Humberto López Tristán, Javier Henríquez Lara
Photography: David Jilkyns
Illustrator: Humberto López Tristán
Client: Joselo

Client wanted to create a different coffee franchise. Starting with the brand's name, he was looking for a personal experience and the idea of someone behind every aspect of the service.

In order to contain brand personality designers created a typeface that could express both politeness and expertise with textures and auxiliary elements. Auxiliary font Gotham completes the artisanal sense of the brand with a current and fresh look, reinforcing brand differentiation and character. Its irregular size communicates relaxation and solidity with a treatment that also reflects elegance and professionalism.

Colour Scheme

Primary

C0 M86 Y80 K0
R247 G64 B58
#F7403A

Secondary

C0 M0 Y0 K100
R30 G30 B30
#1E1E1E

Logo in Grid / Diagram

Fonts used: Typography created especially for the brand; Gotham as Auxiliary Source
Typeface Styles: Modified Serif in logo; Sans-Serif as Auxiliary Font

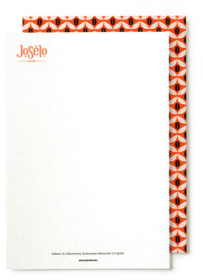

Dusk & Dawn

Project Manager & Copywriter: Lia Caldeira
Art Director: Lia Caldeira
Designer: Lia Caldeira
Illustrator: Lia Caldeira
Client: Carolina Martins, Dusk & Dawn

The goal was to design a logo for a handmade crafts store called Dusk & Dawn that specialises in custom crafts for home décor and weddings.

Since it's a very emotional and artisanal brand, the designer decided to create an emotional look by designing a hand lettered script font, a delicate flower crown illustration and by choosing candid colours. The colours specifically were inspired by the pink and purple colours of the sky during dusk and dawn.

Colour Scheme

Primary

C62 M31 Y40 K12

C0 M37 Y19 K0

C5 M55 Y27 K0

C0 M69 Y38 K0

Logo in Grid / Diagram

Fonts used: Custom Designed Typeface; Claire Hand (Modified)
Typeface Styles: Sans-Serif; Script

Matchaki

Design Agency: Monajans
Art Director: Mustafa Akülker
Designer: Mustafa Akülker
Illustrator: Mustafa Akülker
Client: Matchaki

Matchaki is a type of green tea made by taking young tea leaves and grinding them into a bright green powder. This is different from regular green tea, where the leaves are infused in water, then removed. Matchaki is one of the organisations that promote matcha in NewYork.

Designer used the green colour in branding work by going out of the way of Matcha tea and keeping the memorability. Based on the Matcha leaf, designer created typography from the letter M and used it on the body. At the same time designer created a pattern for this logo with dark and light green of green tones as corporate colours. The logo is also used in different materials, such as paper-ceramic cups, teapots, paper bags, as well as in the use of stationary products and in various cold service units. It is very important to reflect the elegance for the target audience, so it is a contemporary and cool design for a drinking as the brand.

Colour Scheme

Primary

C89 M44 Y76 K45
R7 G75 B58
#074b3a

C66 M0 Y85 K0
R80 G197 B93
#50c55d

Secondary

C2 M2 Y2 K0
R249 G245 B244
#f9f5f4

Logo in Grid / Diagram

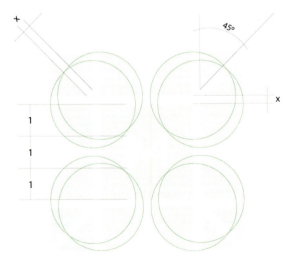

Fonts used: Adieu Regular; Andale Mono
Typeface Style: Sans-Serif

MATCHAKI

Somos

Art Director: Tomomi Maezawa
Designer: Tomomi Maezawa
Client: Somos

Somos is an Ecuadorian NGO that fights against social inequality in the crafts industries. They asked designer to create an identity that not only expresses traditional humanity and sustainability of the brand but also attracts a contemporary audience beyond the local context.

The visual response was a simple and clean shape representing the people who collaborate hand in hand, embracing the Ecuadorian landscape. The word "SOMOS" is hidden in the shape, making the mark more unique. Inspired by the nature and culture of Ecuador, the delicate colour palette aims to gets away from the stereotypical South American aesthetics. Simple, clean and sleek typeface to attract the contemporary design market rather than the ethnic and touristic representation of the culture.

Designer wanted people to see the logo like a stamp on a postcard. When the logo is printed or engraved on their products, the logo makes the products feel like a warm greeting from the place. The logo assembles the letters, "SOMOS", while the letters envelop the drawing to be as one symbol.

Colour Scheme

Primary

C85 M61 Y50 K51
R38 G59 B69

Secondary

C71 M49 Y67 K53
R57 G71 B58

C14 M29 Y34 K2
R220 G186 B165

C15 M7 Y21 K0
R226 G228 B210

C17 M16 Y21 K1
R217 G210 B201

C54 M56 Y62 K61
R75 G62 B52

Logo in Grid / Diagram

Fonts used: Raisonne; Apercu
Typeface Style: Sans-Serif

Komorebi Architecture Studio

Design Agency: Dmentes Estudio Creativo
Project Manager & Copywriter: Ángel González Blanco
Art Director: Eva Canal Pesquera
Designer: Carlos Iglesias González
Client: Komorebi

Komorebi is an architecture minimalist studio with a great interest in nature and light within his buildings. Komorebi, is a Japanese word which refers to the light that filters through the leaves. The light converts into a geometric figure like an architectural structure.

The typography used in the logo is Helvetica, a minimalist font with a polished structure to make the greatest efficiency with minimal details like the minimalist architecture. To simulate the light on the logo, the characters that enter on the geometric form are in a negative colour, simulating being backlighting.

Colour Scheme

Primary

C0 M14 Y15 K10
Pantone P 42-9C

Secondary

C0 M0 Y0 K95
Pantone P 179-15C

C0 M0 Y0 K75

Logo in Grid / Diagram

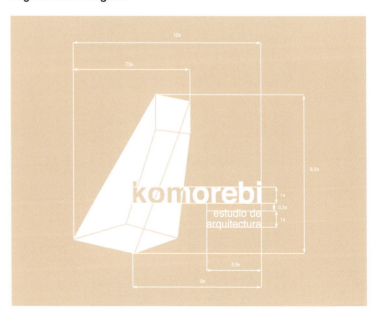

Font used: Helvetica
Typeface Style: Sans-Serif

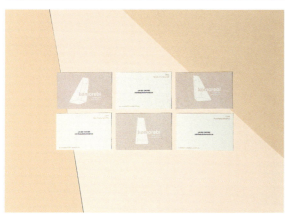

Saint Joy Rebranding

Design Agency: Juke Creative Studio

Art Director: Christophe Branchu, Julien Gueuning

Designer: Christophe Branchu, Julien Gueuning, Arnaud Le Devehat, Archer Zuo

Client: Saint Joy

Saint Joy was founded in 1889. They pursue a long tradition inherited from the Song Dynasty of Chinese Brocade production. The challenge of redesigning their visual identity was to keep the brand's heritage while modernnising its image and being globally attractive.

The Chinese font is based on traditional Song style. For the English logo, designers designed a serif font to express heritage that matches with the Chinese typography. They added an ornament inspired by Song brocade in the letter "O" to enhance its identity while keeping it modern. The auxiliary icons enhance the overall identity while making the brand more international. The main icon represents a front facing brocade looming machine. The overall shape has an architectural construction with strong perspective lines that evocate a building. Inspiration comes from Western historical brands that are often associated with "house" incarnating history which helps to understand their brand heritage.

They also designed a secondary smaller icon representing a shuttle to evocate the handwork necessary for looming as well a pattern based on the traditional geometrics found in Song Dynasty.

Colour Scheme

Primary

C67 M64 Y66 K64
R49 G45 B42
#312D2A

Secondary

C21 M19 Y25 K0
R203 G196 B185
#CBC4B9

C0 M0 Y0 K0
R255 G255 B255
#FFFFFF

Logo in Grid / Diagram

Font used: Original

Typeface Style: Serif

SAINT JOY
上 久 楷

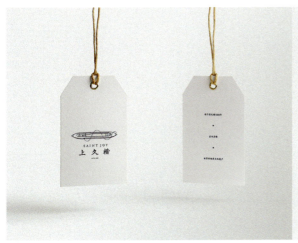

Xocola Organic Chocolate

Project Manager & Copywriter: Kimmy Lee
Art Director: Kimmy Lee
Designer: Kimmy Lee

Born from the desire to create the simplest and purest "bean-to-bar" confectionery, Xocola is one of only a handful of micro-batch makers of premium and fair trade chocolates. Xocola only uses organic, high-quality ingredients combined with non-roasting techniques to bring out the truest and purest cacao flavours.

Typography
It is a clean, simple, pretty straightforward serif logo; the contrast of the thick and thin lines provides a nice balance and boldness to the overall aesthetic, while the pointy termination of the serif hints at the sharp edges of the chocolate bar and box.

Colour Scheme

Primary

C75 M68 Y67 K90
R0 G0 B0
#000000

Secondary

C0 M6 Y88 K0
R255 G240 B31
#FFFF01F

C0 M0 Y0 K0
R255 G255 B255
#FFFFFF

Fonts used: Giaza Pro; Brandon Grotesque
Typeface Styles: Serif; Sans-Serif

Colour Palette

Focusing on the aspects of contrast and balance, the yellow is used as an accent colour, lending a bright contrast to the deep-brown chocolate bar while adding a playful pop of colour to the black and white design.

Pattern

The stylised illustration takes its cue from the shape of the cacao fruit and its leaves; keeping it very organic than geometric, with fluid lines for a softer impression; the splatter takes its cue from the irregular shapes of broken cacao nibs/shards.

Toothopia Kids' Dentist

Designer: AguWu

The Toothopia project consists of a logo and illustrations created for a private dentist practice in California. The main goal was to design a message understandable for little patients of the practice and this was achieved by using geometric shapes, vibrant colour palette and short, cheerful phrases. It was paramount to divert a child's attention from a stressful appointment and to show that caring for their smile can be great fun. The logo represents a girl and a boy in a simplified, geometric form corresponding to a shape of a circle or letter "O" which makes it playful. The characters are combined with simple shapes and happy phrases to create illustrations.

Colour Scheme

Primary

R255 G179 B151
#ffb397

R0 G158 B255
#009eff

Fonts used: Cera Basic; Cera PRO Bold
Typeface Style: Sans-Serif

Lemon Hotel

Design Agency: Takram
Creative Director: Kotaro Watanabe
Designer: Tomomi Maezawa
Photography: Kotaro Yamaguchi, Terushige Enatsu
Client: Smiles

Lemon Hotel is an art installation and accommodation at Setouchi Triennale produced by Smiles.

Setouchi Triennale is an international art festival held on several islands in the Seto Inland Sea of Japan. The festival invites artists from both Japan and overseas, many of whom make use of abandoned homes to host their art installations.

The challenge was to create a symbol that strikes a chord with both national and international visitors. The result is a bilingual typography whose Japanese scripts are modelled after Western cursive form. Its incomplete lines suggest a shape of lemon in a response to the concept of the installation celebrating the pure and sour taste of distant memories.

Colour Scheme

Primary

C0 M0 Y0 K0
R255 G255 B255
#FFFFFF

C86 M51 Y71 K54
R20 G62 B52
#033f34

Initial Sketches   Western-inspired Cursive Script

Draft   Font Solutions

Font used: Circular
Typeface Style: Script

Sensory Artisan — Geisha Collection

Design Agency: Never-Never
Design Director: Woody Chau
Art Director: Can Chan
Illustrator: Can Chan
Client: Sensory Artisan

Geisha illustration is designed for the coffee-beer product. Idea comes from the name of main ingredient : Geisha Bean. It is interesting that the name also stand for Japanese women who study the ancient tradition of art. In the graphics, designers use waves and Japanese Geisha as the main elements. The former represents the challenges and the power of beer. The Door God tatto at the back of geisha is a hints of crossover beer company — Moonzen Brewery.

Colour Scheme

Primary

C40 M30 Y30 K100

Pantone 871C

C0 M0 Y0 K0

Font used: Original
Typeface Style: Japanese Calligraphy

Wukungfu

Design Agency: Siwei Design
Project Manager & Copywriter: Lai Siwei
Art Director: Lai Siwei
Designer: Lai Siwei
Client: Wukungfu

Wukungfu is a Chinese martial arts teaching studio. With twenty years of martial arts teaching experience, it aims to transform the essence of martial arts into a life attitude. For this reason, the client hopes to inspire people's different viewpoints from the new brand identification and derive different understandings of martial arts. In the logo design, it is necessary to keep the intuitive sense to martial arts, so designers use calligraphy as the medium to convey a first impression to people — poised. However, different from other projects, the planning of the structure is no longer limited to the Chinese characters and calligraphy only acts as a simple medium, because people's impression of the movements in martial arts is presented by "drawing and writing".

Returning to the original intention, Wukungfu hopes people start martial arts intentionally and then end a day with a light heart. So the final image may look like the Chinese character " 心 " (heart), or a person lying comfortably, or even a strong movement in martial arts. Starting from the "heart", they hope to get more diverse viewpoints from different perspectives. All in all, Wushu, or Chinese martial arts, is not only a serious and formal ancient art, but also an introverted dance. It even has no fixed postures, but another attitude towards life.

Colour Scheme*

Primary

C0 M0 Y0 K100

C42 M100 Y100 K9

Font used: Original
Typeface Styles: Others

CONTRIBUTORS

ARTPOWER

Acknowledgements

We would like to thank all the designers and companies who made significant contributions to the compilation of this book. Without them, this project would not have been possible. We would also like to thank many others whose names did not appear on the credits, but made specific input and support for the project from beginning to end.

Future Editions

If you would like to contribute to the next edition of Artpower, please email us your details to: artpower@artpower.com.cn